The PATHER PANCHALI

Sketchbook

SATYAJIT RAY

The PATHER PANCHALI Sketchbook

Edited by SANDIP RAY

in association with

Arup K. De, Deepak Mukerjee, Debasis Mukhopadhyay

Foreword by DHRITIMAN CHATERJI

Introduction by SHARMILA TAGORE

Harper Collins

Society for the Preservation of Satyajit Ray Archives

First published in India in 2016 by HarperCollins *Publishers* India
4th Floor, Tower A, Building No. 10, Phase II, DLF Cyber City,
Gurugram, Haryana – 122002
www.harpercollins.co.in

In association with
Society for the Preservation of Satyajit Ray Archives

P-ISBN for PB edition: 978-93-5177-933-9
P-ISBN for PLC edition: 978-81-7223-778-3
E-ISBN: 978-93-5177-934-6

2 4 6 8 10 9 7 5 3

Cover design and book layout by **Pinaki De**

Printed and bound at
Nutech Print Services - India

পথের পাঁচালী

Pather Panchali, film title calligraphy by Satyajit Ray

CONTENTS

PREFACE

SANDIP RAY

Member Secretary,
Society for the Preservation of Satyajit Ray Archives

The first time I saw *Pather Panchali* was in 1955. I was about two years old at the time. My mother took me to one of the movie theatres in south Kolkata where the film had released on 26 August 1955. Naturally, I retain little memory of that viewing.

But I saw the film a number of times later on. People who came to meet my father from afar would often want to see it. So we had to organize private screenings for them, mostly in studios. *Pather Panchali* moved me to tears whenever I saw it, even when I watched it at the Museum of Modern Art in New York on 4 May last year. The museum ran a new-look *Pather Panchali*, restored by the Criterion Collection and the L'Immagine Ritrovata in Bologna, Italy, to relive the world premiere of the film that had taken place at the same place sixty years ago, on 3 May 1955.

Father introduced a novelty for *Pather Panchali* to allure prospective producers. He did not use his now-famous *kheror khata* (red notebook) to write the screenplay. In fact, there was no fully formed conventional script for the film. He did some sketches in a drawing book after he had come back from London in 1950 and illustrated a succession of pictures (in pen, brush and ink) for the sequences of frames as they would come up in the film. He used to take them to the producers and explain the sequences. The producers he approached, however, had no interest, nor could they understand the whole process.

I never saw him look back, except on one occasion when he expressed mild regrets about the first half of *Pather Panchali*. That was when the National Film Development Corporation (NFDC) released the film on videocassettes. Dulal Dutta, his editor, was there at our home the day the NFDC people came to present us a complimentary copy of the cassette. We were all very excited and ran it on our machine. While watching the film, father remarked that he would have done some repairing if he had got an opportunity to work on the film again at the editing table.

What father meant was that relative inexperience had prevented him from handling *Pather Panchali*, or, precisely speaking, the first part of the film, with greater care and skill. He was then a virtual stranger to the world of film-making. In fact, he was more or less satisfied about the second half of the film. It was the first part that he found a bit slack and sprawling in patches.

Father did some of his shot divisions on cigarette packs and chits of paper which he passed on to Subrata Mitra, his cinematographer, during shooting. I have no idea if any other director did their shot divisions so painstakingly and exhaustively in those days or does so now. I later asked Mitra if he had preserved any of the *Pather Panchali* sketches he had received from father. Unfortunately, he said he had not.

Coming back to the *Pather Panchali* sketchbook. Father donated it to the Cinémathèque Français in Paris at the request of Georges Sadoul, the eminent French journalist and film scholar. In his final days, he expressed a desire to have a look at the visual script he had made for *Pather Panchali*. I contacted the Cinémathèque Français management, but they said the sketchbook had been missing. However, it was our good luck that last year we got hold of a scanned copy of it through the good offices of the Criterion Collection and decided to bring out this facsimile edition. We intend to make the book a dossier on *Pather Panchali*.

It is the first time that the admirers of Satyajit Ray around the world will get an opportunity to have a look at the entire sketchbook which formed the very foundation on which father made his maiden film.

Kolkata, March 2016

FOREWORD

DHRITIMAN CHATERJI

Dhritiman Chaterji, one of Satyajit Ray's favourite actors, played the lead role in *Pratidwandi* (The Adversary). He also appeared in two other films by Ray, *Ganashatru* (An Enemy of the People) and *Agantuk* (The Stranger).

NOTES TO HIMSELF

If Satyajit Ray had not died an untimely death at seventy-one, he might have gone on to make a film featuring Felu Mitter called *Panchali Rohoshyo* or *The Mystery of Pather Panchali*. Three-and-a-half decades after it was made, *Pather Panchali* was rife with mystery and high drama.

In his last days, Ray expressed a wish to see the *Pather Panchali* sketchbook, which he had donated to the Cinémathèque Français archives in Paris. But the sketchbook had gone missing. Fortunately, said the Cinémathèque, they had made a copy which they could send.

Soon after his death, the family discovered that the final draft of his account of making the film, *My Years with Apu*, had been stolen from his study. An earlier draft was found, salvaged and prepared for publication with loving care by his wife.

> 'I can never forget the excitement in my mind after seeing it [*Pather Panchali*]. It is the kind of cinema that flows with the serenity and nobility of a big river.' — **Akira Kurosawa**

More was to follow. Just about a year after his death, the negative of *Pather Panchali* was being shipped to Los Angeles for restoration via a London laboratory. In July 1993, all of a sudden, there was a fire in the lab and the negative suffered serious damage.

In spite of these mysterious and unfortunate events, it has been possible to recreate the world of *Pather Panchali* in this book, sixty years after the film was made. The book is the result of a long and patient archiving effort, to which a number of people have made valuable contributions. It can be argued that creative people are too busy creating to think of preserving their work for posterity. Others have to do it for them.

The book will be of value to all kinds of readers. Film scholars and Ray enthusiasts will find a wealth of material in one place: the sketchbook itself, parts of the draft scenario, reviews, recollections, posters and illustrations. Equally important, younger filmgoers, including those who might not even have seen the film yet, will see a process unfolding, a mind at work. With the media barrage that the young are subjected to today (or subject themselves to!), perhaps it needs an extra little push to persuade them to visit one of the greatest artistic works of all time. This book could be that push.

Let me interject a personal recollection here. When we were shooting the public meeting scene in *Ganashatru*, Ray did a tracking shot of Soumitra Chatterjee and me from left to right. After the shot, the cinematographer asked whether they should set up for the reverse angle. Ray was very sure in his reply: 'No, I've got what I wanted.' Being sure, being precise and being in control over all aspects of making a film are characteristics that Ray has been reputed for.

The sketchbook, looked at together with his recollections of making the film in *My Years with Apu*, shows that certainty and precision were not qualities that came to him as a matter of divine right. They were acquired through a deep study of cinema (including seeing ninety-nine films in six months when he was in England!), clarity about his own aesthetic, artistic and, indeed, social and political positions, and a process of probing, learning, experimenting and innovating in the company of a small, inexperienced but dedicated group of co-workers who were as committed to this process as he was.

And, of course, the entire process began with Santiniketan, Rabindranath and the masters Nandalal Bose and Benode Behari Mukherjee. The illustrations for *Aam Aantir Bhenpu*, the abridged version of *Pather Panchali* published by Signet Press, for example,

An illustration by Ray from *Aam Aantir Bhenpu*

which so fired our imagination when we were children, already indicate a cinematic sensibility. Ray's cinema of humanism was not merely an artistic construct. It derived organically from the way his family traditions and Santiniketan shaped him as a human being.

The sketchbook is precious to the world of cinema because, quite simply, it shows us how one of the greatest films we've ever seen was visualized. I personally have no way of knowing why Ray chose this way of working. I talked about many things with him but the sketchbook was somehow missed out in our conversations. I can only surmise.

The first thing, of course, is that Ray was an illustrator and it was perhaps natural that he should choose to lay out in pictures an end product that would be realized in pictures. Secondly, I think, he wanted to predetermine as precisely as possible what he would shoot. And this for two reasons. One was simply that it was in his nature to be precise. The other, I feel, was a very practical reason: economy. He knew that he would have to make the film with very little money and that second thoughts, improvisations, multiple takes, etc., on set and location would be difficult.

When I study the sketchbook now, I see Ray trying to do four things with it. First, outlining the narrative sequence. Second, getting a sense of the individual characters. Third, searching for a feel of pace, movement and scene transitions (at one place, he writes 'Dissolve' and then crosses it out). Incidentally, in the sketchbook, 'dissolve' seems to be his favourite mode of transition. I'm not at all sure that the edited film had as many dissolves as the sketchbook does! And fourth, placing the whole enterprise in a physical context – ponds, fields, railway tracks, sunsets…

As the sketchbook progresses, he seems to become increasingly sure about what he's doing or what he intends to use the sketchbook for. He uses fewer words to annotate his frames until, two-thirds of the way through, words cease altogether and a visual narrative ebbs and flows to its conclusion. What the technically inclined will also notice is that an unselfconscious visual grammar starts to manifest itself – crisp, uncluttered framing, an awareness of foreground-background juxtaposition and, very importantly, an even, natural, understated lighting style made vivid by his mastery of pen, ink and brush illustrations. I also find the fact that he uses only a few scraps of dialogue in the entire sketchbook very interesting. His aversion to the dialogue-heavy, overly 'literary' Bengali cinema of the time is well-known. Was outlining a film in pictures rather than in words a way of reminding himself that cinema stays true to a work of literature not by translating it, but by transforming it?

Historians and chroniclers often like to play the 'what if' game. What if Ray had not come from such a distinguished lineage? What if he had not had the skills to produce a sketchbook that brought his proposed film to life? What if he had not found such an unlikely backer as the chief minister of West Bengal? Would *Pather Panchali* ever have got made? Who knows?

What we do know is that going back to the roots of one of the greatest films ever made takes us inside the mind of its maker, makes us privy to the notes that, more than six decades ago, he made to himself.

INTRODUCTION

SHARMILA TAGORE

Sharmila Tagore is regarded as one of India's finest actors. She debuted in the third part of Ray's Apu trilogy, *Apur Sansar*, and went on to act in four more films directed by Ray. She was one of the most popular actors in Hindi cinema of the 1970s.

Writing an introduction to *Pather Panchali* is challenging. What is there to say about the film that has not already been said? For sixty years now, film-makers, critics, scholars, academics and lovers of cinema the world over have discussed, debated and analysed the film for its sheer brilliance and simple intensity. Through his haunting images and memorable characters, Ray built a bridge between his beloved Bengal and the rest of the world, and I have often stood on that bridge. It is equally heart-warming to experience how people from different cultures, old and young, respond to *Pather Panchali*, and the questions they ask. The Academy, despite restoring the Apu trilogy, had never screened it in Los Angeles until recently. I was invited as a special guest and for me attending the event was an overwhelming experience. The audience loved the film and long after it was over, the sense of wonder remained.

Pather Panchali has a hugely significant place in world cinema and, in particular, in Indian cinema and that fact has been reinforced as each decade has gone by. It is the only Indian film that regularly features in a list of Top 100 films of all times compiled by film critics and international magazines. The Criterion Collection has recently released a dazzlingly restored version of the Apu trilogy which will hopefully attract and introduce the films to a new generation. Even sixty years after it was made, *Pather Panchali*, the first of the trilogy, continues to be part of our discourse, our consciousness, seen and admired across cultures and countries. This book is testimony to that.

The film holds a special place in my heart. In fact, I can say this without a doubt: I owe my life in cinema to this film. In the 1950s, cinema was frowned upon by the middle-class and intellectual elite in Bengal. Even watching a film was actively discouraged, leave alone acting in one! *Pather Panchali* changed all that. Interestingly enough, I find a similar sentiment in a couple of articles in this book. Subrata Mitra's fascinating essay dwells on this. As does Subir Banerjee's memory piece on the *only* film he has acted in. Without any exaggeration, it can be said that *Pather Panchali* made cinema in Bengal 'respectable'.

I remember vividly the anticipation that had built up weeks before the film was released. Our joint family household was abuzz with excited speculation about the film and its maker. The son of Sukumar Ray, grandson of Upendrakishore Ray Chowdhury, had at last made a film good enough for our children. I finally watched the film with my cousins and I was totally engrossed. I felt distraught when Durga was being punished, shocked by the naughty things she got up to, and somewhat envious of her free spirit. I did not have a clue that three years on, I would be on that big screen and others would be watching me.

No doubt impressed with the resounding international success of *Pather Panchali* and the critical acclaim for its maker, my father took the extraordinary step of allowing me to work in *Apur Sansar*. He realized the significance of the Apu trilogy. But my school didn't, and my principal asked me to leave in case my very presence in the classroom corrupted young minds.

But I digress ... that was sixty years ago, the years seem to have gone by so quickly. And yet, even after all this time, the film remains vibrant in my memory. I can still hear Pandit Ravi Shankar's achingly haunting music; see the white kaash flowers gently swaying in the autumn breeze; anticipate the sweetmeat seller with his lilting gait as he walks down the village path, the salivating kids in tow; admire the glistening dragonflies pirouetting on the shimmering pond; feel unsettled by Indir Thakrun's death and devastated by the destruction of Apu's

> '*Pather Panchali*, the first film by Satyajit Ray, became a classic of Indian cinema. I, along with many others, still think that *Pather Panchali* is one of his best creations. Though it may be technically less perfect than his later films, it has a naturalness, a lyricism, a spontaneity and a charming look of sophistication that combine to give the film a beautiful unity.' — **Pandit Ravi Shankar**

home and its courtyard. I relive the scene where Apu throws away the necklace that Durga had stolen and how the village pond gathers it up and forever hides Durga's transgression.

Akira Kurosawa found 'Ray's quiet but deep observation, understanding and love of the human race' very moving. He felt that 'Ray's was the kind of cinema that flows with the serenity and nobility of a big river. People are born, live out their lives and then accept their death without the least effort and without any sudden jerks. Its effect on the audience is to stir up deep passions.' All this is true of *Pather Panchali*.

'To one who has seen Part One [of the Apu Trilogy], two things are now evident. The film now seems better than it did because the second was made, and the director, Mr Ray, is in the process of creating a national film epic unlike anything in size and soul since the Soviet Maxim trilogy of 1938-40. Further, as a record of a people's life, in its daily travail and its largest aspects, it bears comparison with Flaherty's *Nanook* and *Maona*.' — **Stanley Kauffman**

The fifty-eight-page storyboard brings the film alive in another form. Leafing through the pages, I can see Ray's meticulous attention to every detail, how closely his illustrations approximate what we see on-screen. It is astonishing to see how clear he was about what he wanted, despite being a first-time director. The sketchbook is a veritable manual for the aspiring film-maker, particularly for those who wish to express themselves through images while liberating scenes from excessive dialogue.

At the same time, the book is also a collector's edition because of what it contains: parts of the draft scenario, insightful reviews, memory pieces, posters and illustrations. Many English-language readers will get to read, probably for the first time, essays by stalwarts like Subrata Mitra and Bansi Chandragupta.

I congratulate the Society for the Preservation of Satyajit Ray Archives for putting this book together. The publication of the sketchbook that Manik-da used as a reference to make *Pather Panchal* is a significant step in preserving an important slice of cinematic history.

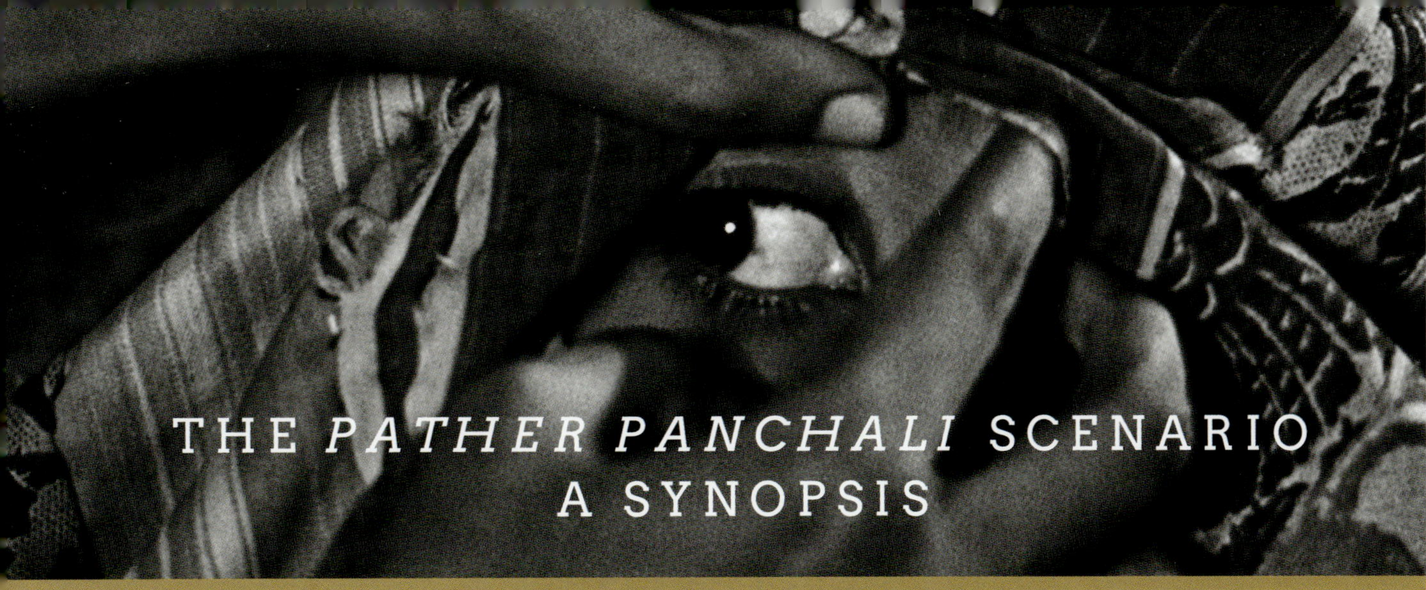

THE *PATHER PANCHALI* SCENARIO A SYNOPSIS

SATYAJIT RAY

Nischindipur – a village on the Ichchhamati river. Mango orchards, bamboo groves, bananas and coconuts, green pond with red and white lotuses and green hyacinths. One of a thousand such villages in Bengal.

Among its predominantly Brahmin population lives Harihar Ray (38) with his family, consisting of his wife Sarbajaya (27), daughter Durga (6) and a distant cousin, Indir Thakrun (80). Before coming to this ancestral village, Harihar had studied the scriptures in Benares. He has a distinct talent for poetry (in the tradition of panchali writers) but has little time for it now as he is trying to settle down. His profession of priesthood is not very paying. But Harihar is essentially an optimist. And he is helped enormously by his wife who is a shrewd and practical woman who can face up to struggle. Old Indir, who lives in a hut of her own in a corner of the courtyard, is unloved and unwanted – except by Durga. Sarba and Indir bicker constantly, and the latter usually ends up by threatening to leave home, which she does, only to be coaxed back in a few days by Durga.

Durga herself goes about stealing fruits from other people's orchards – particularly from those of the rich Mukherjees, their neighbours (their house is still a good five minutes' walk from Harihar's). Mrs Mukherjee (Sejo Thakrun) is a cantankerous woman who does not conceal her disdain for Harihar's family. Sarbajaya rebukes her daughter for stealing but secretly regrets that their own orchards, their only property excepting their house, have been confiscated by the Mukherjees. The only sympathetic friend Sarba has in the village is Nilmani's wife (Na'di).

On a cold night in the month of Magh (January-February), a son is born to Sarbajaya. Harihar is happy. Luckily enough, a few weeks later, Harihar finds a job as a gomasta (rent collector) in the zamindar's treasury. As old Indir rocks the newborn Apu to sleep, singing a lullaby, Harihar sits in the kitchen and plans for the future. 'I know the gomasta's job is a very honourable one and a salary of eight rupees a month is not a good deal of money – but give me two years. In two years we will have settled down, and then everything will be as we wish. We will repair the house, find a husband for Durga and send Apu to a good school. And I shall start writing plays and poems. And then – fame and fortune!' Sarbajaya is infected by her husband's optimism.

SIX YEARS LATER: Harihar is still drudging in the zamindar's treasury … the house looks more dilapidated … Indir and Sarba still bicker and quarrel. Durga, twelve, is now an expert fruit stealer. The boy Apu, pampered by sister and mother, has just started to go to the pathsala (village school). The pathsala has eight other students and is run by a pandit (scholar) who also keeps a grocery store and relies more on the cane than on any textbooks to impart knowledge. Apu, however, is a good pupil and generally manages to escape caning.

Sarbajaya is tired of her husband's complacence and constantly reminds him of his promises and his ambition. 'At least try to assert yourself at the zamindar's and insist that they pay you regularly, if not handsomely. This way we shall soon begin to starve…'

One afternoon, while Sarba is feeding Apu, there is a sudden invasion by Sejo Thakrun and her two daughters. They charge in and demand to see Durga. Sarbajaya, taken aback, asks what has happened. Sejo accuses Durga of having made off with her daughter Penchi's necklace that very afternoon. Durga arrives, is searched, but the necklace is not found on her person. Sejo, frustrated, lets loose her tongue and bitterly accuses Sarbajaya of pettiness, corruption and downright thievery. Then she leaves as dramatically as she came. Sarba, hurt and humiliated beyond words, vents her rage on Durga and literally throws her out of the house. Indir intervenes, only to be rebuked. Apu watches horrified. After a while, Sarba realizes the extent of her cruelty, asks Apu to go and find Durga and fetch her, which duty the boy performs only too gladly.

That night (it is the month of Bhadra – August-September), when Indir tells a fairy tale to the two children, Harihar returns home with three months' pay (which had been due) and good news: the offer of an initiation ceremony in a rich peasant family. 'Have you accepted it?' asks Sarba breathlessly. 'Not so soon. It is wrong to show too much eagerness in such matters. I have said I'll give my word in (the month of) Agrahayan (November-December), after the Puja (worship of the goddess Durga).'

While Harihar drowses, Sarbajaya, vexed by her husband's delay in grabbing the opportunity but still prepared to look forward to the future confidently, keeps on muttering to herself: 'I wish we could leave this wretched place. No one respects you here. There is nothing here but poverty and humiliation…'

Just before Puja, Sarbajaya has her bitterest quarrel with Indir. This time the old woman leaves, fully determined never to return.

Puja comes. Apu and Durga, who do not feel the sting of poverty as much as the elders do, enjoy it in their own humble way. Apu's imagination is fired by a jatra (a village theatre) performance, and at home he dresses himself up as a king, having helped himself to knick-knacks and ornaments from her sister's box. Durga discovers the theft (Apu's) and the two have a fight. Durga pretends to be piqued and runs away, out of the village, along the river, across the meadows of the paddy fields. Apu follows desperately, afraid that he would lose his sister's friendship. On the edge of an unknown kaash field, the two are reconciled, and their long journey is rewarded by their first, totally unexpected and wondrous glimpse of a railway train.

But old Indir, who has been turned out of the house, returns again. This time she is ill and begs that she be allowed to die in her home. But Sarbajaya, incredulous, sternly refuses. So Indir has to leave again, tottering.

Apu and Durga, returning from their sight of the train, catch sight of Indir lying beside a bamboo grove. They move close to her, gladdened by the discovery of their beloved aunt. But Durga, wiser and older of the two, realizes with a shock that Indir is dead.

'I must admit I get rather restive when people write saying that my first published story was my best. Perhaps Satyajit feels the same about his own firstborn. But surely *Pather Panchali* is one of the most heartbreakingly beautiful films ever made. There are scenes which I need never view again because they are burnt upon my memory.'— **Arthur C. Clarke**

AGRAHAYAN: As planned, Harihar sets out for the initiation ceremony at the rich peasant's. 'I shall be back in a week's time,' he says, 'and with the money I will have earned, I shall get the house repaired. It is doubtful if it will last through another monsoon without repair.'

Sarba prepares for their coming prosperity.

But what is this? A postcard from Harihar!

And it is disastrous news. The rich peasant has suffered two deaths in the family through malaria. No question of initiation now. Harihar is proceeding to the city where by reading from the scriptures he will earn enough for the repairs and thereupon return.

Sarbajaya, shaken at first, realizes that weakening will make matters worse, and decides to face whatever is in store for them.

Days run into weeks, and weeks into months. Winter comes and goes, but there is no letter from Harihar. The Mukherjees' oldest daughter, the charming and gentle Ranu (a favourite of Durga), gets married. The wedding touches Durga who realizes for the first time that she will also one day get married and have children. She begins to take more care for herself and performs the bratas she has so far neglected. Apu finds his thirst for knowledge growing, and along with it grows his sense of wonder and curiosity.

But their poverty grows too. Sarbajaya finds herself fighting a losing battle, and begins to sell and pawn her possessions secretly. But Nilmani's wife finds out and generously offers that Sarba should accept help from them. Sarba, reluctant at first, is later forced to accept.

25th OF CHAITRA (MARCH-APRIL): Like a ray of light in the ever-increasing gloom comes Harihar's postcard. Good news! He has collected the necessary amount and will be returning home in a week. Sarbajaya sheds tears of joy.

1st OF BAISHAKH (APRIL-MAY): As Durga performs the punyipukur brata, suddenly, without warning, comes the first Kalbaishakhi (nor'wester) storm of the season. Durga leaves her brata, runs out and meets Apu at the mango orchard where they joyously collect mangoes fallen from trees which had once belonged to them. Then comes the rain. Durga, deliriously happy, makes for the open spaces and gets thoroughly drenched, while Apu, less adventurous, takes shelter under a tree.

Durga catches a cold which develops into pneumonia. The village doctor tries his best – which is really not much.

On a terribly stormy night, Durga dies in her mother's arms.

For six days and six nights, Sarbajaya remains like one petrified, while Apu wanders about, bewildered and lonely.

On the **10th OF BAISHAKH,** Harihar returns. The disaster that meets him stirs him to the bottom of his heart. It also makes a new man of him.

As the house is damaged beyond repair, Harihar decides to leave Nischindipur and try his luck in Benares. This is not what he had hoped for, but he accepts his fate (in spite of being discouraged by his neighbours) in a realistic manner.

Two important incidents occur on the day before their departure. Sejo Thakrun has a change of heart and brings Sarbajaya a basketful of mangoes for their journey. And Apu discovers, in a corner of the dust-laden shelf, the necklace belonging to Penchi! This he promptly throws into the nearby pond.

On the **25th OF BAISHAKH,** at dawn, Harihar leaves his ancestral home with his wife and son. As the rickety bullock cart lumbers down the muddy village road, the rising sun is seen through the clouds for the first time after a long stretch of gloomy days.

'... It [*Pather Panchali*] has enough merits to be considered as a film event just as the book in literary field. ... This vital, moving and emotionally compact picture can only indicate how patiently and meticulously the director had prepared himself before he put his hand to the book. ... The few studio sets made by Bansi Chandragupta, in which interior sequences are continued, are so faithful that the transition is hardly noticed. Subrata Mitra's photography does not merely keep perfect pace with the subject. Many of the compositions reveal his or, more truly, his and the director's artistry. The recordist's job has been very arduous and commendable despite unsatisfactory sound projection. ... Talking of musical effect in the film, what Ravi Shankar has achieved with a few simple Indian instruments and occasionally with unaccompanied shaky treble of an old woman's voice has had hardly a parallel in Indian films. Of the cast, the first to be named is Chunibala.'
— Review extract from *The Statesman*, Calcutta, 28 August 1955

'... It is absurd to compare it [*Pather Panchali*] with any other Indian picture — for even the best of the pictures produced so far have been cluttered with clichés. *Pather Panchali* is pure cinema. ... [It] makes a complete break with the world of make-believe. ... He [Satyajit Ray] composes his shots with a virtuosity which he shares with only a few directors in the entire history of cinema.'
— *The Times of India*, 11 February 1956

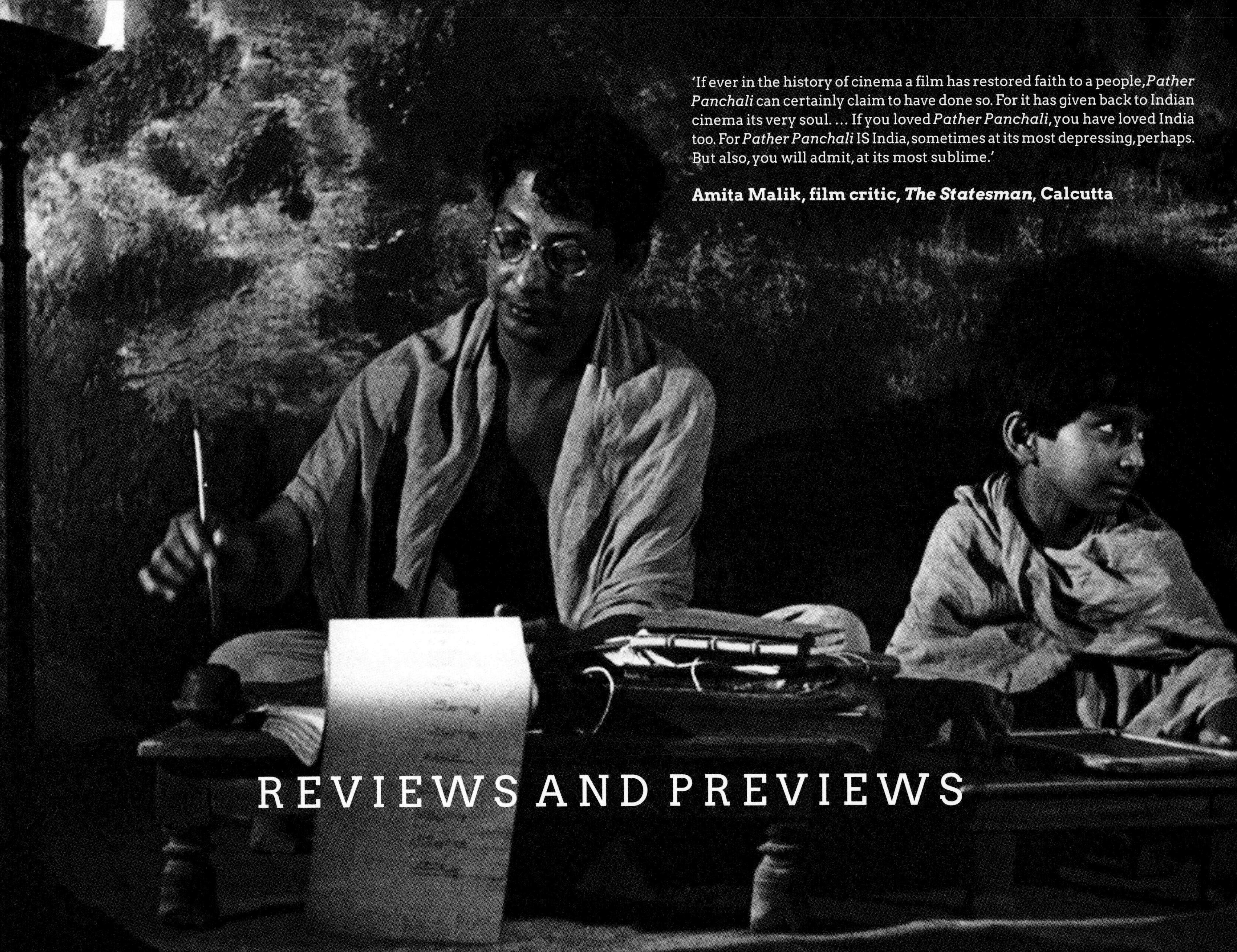

'If ever in the history of cinema a film has restored faith to a people, *Pather Panchali* can certainly claim to have done so. For it has given back to Indian cinema its very soul. ... If you loved *Pather Panchali*, you have loved India too. For *Pather Panchali* IS India, sometimes at its most depressing, perhaps. But also, you will admit, at its most sublime.'

Amita Malik, film critic, *The Statesman*, Calcutta

REVIEWS AND PREVIEWS

A Bold Venture in Many Respects*

When a realistic story of the soil written by an author of repute and read by millions is made into a film, do picture-goers prefer stars or unknown actors to play the characters? This has become a burning question to many producers and directors.

A creative director with conviction believes that realism is lost when attention is given more to the star cast than to the characters in the story. With this in mind, Satyajit Ray, so long known as a genius in commercial art, has brought to the screen Bibhutibhushan Banerjee's immortal story, *Pather Panchali*, with a cast of mostly unknown performers.

Produced by the Government of West Bengal and directed by Satyajit Ray, *Pather Panchali* is a bold venture in many respects. The characters are mostly played by unknown actors. To give real atmosphere to the story, the major portion of the film has been shot outdoors in a village and the players had no recourse to make-up. In some of the sequences it is reported that to give proper effect the artistes had to play their parts amidst the natural rainfall and these scenes have been photographed more beautifully than generally achieved from mechanically made rain.

The music has been composed by the celebrated musician Ravi Shankar and the sets have been designed and constructed by Bansi Chandragupta. The picture will be released today at Basusree, Bina, Chhaya and Sree through Aurora Film Corporation Ltd.

* This preview appeared in *The Statesman, Calcutta*, on 26 August 1955

A Film of Exquisite Beauty*

D.R.M. (Niranjan Majumdar)

Let it be said quite clearly, and right at the outset, that this is no ordinary film we are reviewing. The caution is necessary, because so extravagant is the use of superlatives in film writing in general that words, adjectives in particular, have had their full meaning corroded away, as if by inflation. Every word in this review is to be taken at its full value.

This is the first Indian film which is Indian in every inch. We emphasize this aspect not because it has no universal appeal; it has, but because this film is a truer picture of life in an Indian village than any we have seen. The story is well known; it relates to a Bengal village which is dying out – the sort of village we have all seen and turned away from. It is to such a spot that the young director, Satyajit Ray, has taken his camera, his seeing eye, his feeling heart, and his very capable hands. The result is a film of exquisite beauty, and it is, in the fullest sense of the term, a work of art – a thing we would not say about many films made anywhere.

It has been said once before in this column, it is not in drama that the Bengali film will ever come near its foreign competitors. Life in this part of the world is harsh, painful – but rarely violent. It is the emotions which are occasionally, and only occasionally, violent. What is more in tune with the soil of Bengal is the poetic quality of our nature, human and physical. It is the poetic quality of our landscape, mental and physical, which has been triumphantly caught by director Ray. The characters in the film – Indir Thakrun, Apu, Durga, Sarbajaya and others – are all portrayed beautifully, and Durga is just superb – and having said that, we will go on to add that never is the human element allowed to dominate the film. That would indeed have been false, for in life too, the characters are dominated by nature. They are, oftener than not, objects rather than subjects. But all that is sociology.

> 'The magic of *Pather Panchali* lies in the amusing, poignant, or devastating detail of life with which the story is embroidered. There is no other film quite like *Pather Panchali*, for though it has many features that relate it to the documentary story films of the late Robert Flaherty, it stands by itself as perhaps the only attempt realized in cinema to project the psychology of a family and the drama of their lives into the screen without any of the conventional props of feature film productions.' — **Marie Seton, Ray biographer**

Director Ray's approach is poetic and artistic. Some of the compositions – that quivering lotus in the pond on the eve of the rains, for instance – are like painting. The conception of the entire reel covering the onset of the rains in a Bengal village is poetic, and anyone who has known how the rains change the face of the whole countryside will relive that unforgettable experience in the film. A dying Bengal village has never before come to life as it has done in this unique, yes unique, creation. *Pather Panchali* is a thing of beauty from beginning to end, and let us put it quite bluntly that if for any reason this film should not receive the universal acclamation it deserves (in terms of critical praise and in those of box-office returns), we will have forfeited our right to ask for a good film again.

Some misconceptions remain to be removed. The film is sponsored by the Government of West Bengal. But the

* *Hindusthan Standard*, Calcutta, 1955

latter, very wisely, refrains from interfering with the film. There is no propaganda, except what is there in the film. The propaganda is such that it is only a dead heart which will not, after seeing this film, want to do something for India's villages. But let it be clearly understood that the government has not imposed any of its propaganda stuff on the film which is as its director conceived it.

Secondly, let no one fall into the error of thinking that *Pather Panchali* is intended for long-haired, unwashed, coffee-drinking intellectuals who form cinema societies and do not pay the monthly subscription in time. This is a people's film, if ever there has been one. There are certainly scenes and suggestions which can be appreciated the more by those who have some knowledge of film technique – those who have read Eisenstein and seen Flaherty – but there is nothing at all which cannot be enjoyed by those people whose life the film deals with. 'Deal with', did we say? That is a sordid phrase. The film is a piece of poetry, dedicated to the deathless spirit of Bengal, and it is a poem which can be heard and recited by every Bengali. And, being Bengali, it is bound to conquer the rest of India and the whole world. This film, let us aver, marks the Indian film's coming of age. We salute Satyajit Ray and all his comrades who have produced this superb film. Yes, superb.

'The Discovery of the Festival'

Lotte H. Eisner

The author, a celebrated film critic, was one who thought the first prize (Palme d'Or) should have gone to *Pather Panchali* at the Cannes Film Festival in 1956. She wrote so in her report on the festival that began on 23 April and concluded on 10 May that year. Here are a few extracts from her report:

Monday, 23 April: Opening of the festival delayed because of the Monaco wedding which nobody on the 'cote' wants to hear mentioned again.

Monday, 7 May: ...Here is the discovery of the festival: *Lament of the Road* (*Pather Panchali*) from India. A Bengali film by Satyajit Ray, who, incidentally, worked with Jean Renoir on *The River*. Here is great purity and a surprising cinematic lyricism. It is one of those rare works in which nothing seems to happen, but where we feel we are being given a piece of life itself, unembellished, where we see before our eyes people living their daily lives with their small joys and their great affliction. All this without false exoticism, honesty and without exaggerating the facts. The bitter life of a poor family in Bengal: the mother wearing herself out in her daily work, the father a lazy dreamer, and two children who discover their forest and whose greatest delight is to follow their candy-man to see others taste the sweets.

The director did not go looking for beautiful pictures, they came to him quite naturally; his people, who are not professional actors, have an extraordinary presence, simply living their real lives. And, through them, nature comes to life; the landscape and the rains of the monsoon are all part of their destiny.

Satyajit Ray, the Flaherty of Bengal, undertook this film back in 1952, along with a few friends, non-professional like himself, and an amateur photographer. After three months their funds ran out. In 1955 he was able to resume his work with the help of the Government of West Bengal. It is worthy of a grand prize.

Thursday, 10 May: ...Now we learn the *palmares*, the prizes which everyone divulged this afternoon as close secrets. France wins most of them; First Prize (*Palme d'Or*) for Cousteau's *Le Monde du Silence*. The prize for poetic humour goes to the Swedish *Sommarnattens Leende*, and the human document prize to the Indian film, *Pather Panchali* ... As with all awards, there were many regrets, many objections ... I myself would have given two equal prizes to the Cousteau and Clouzot films, and the *Palme d'Or* to the Indian film.

'... Satyajit Ray accentuates the atmospheric rather than the facts. The incidents [of *Pather Panchali*] are very ordinary but they are revealed with a breathtaking spontaneity so that one gradually becomes unaware of watching them through the medium of art: unconsciously life takes over and art no longer exists in the mind of the spectator.'
— *Illustrated Weekly*, Delhi, 1 June 1956

'... Rarely, if ever before, had the people and the soil of the country been so intimately identified and with such unvarnished faithfulness. And the human warmth, the sweet and simple appeal of life as it exists in the typical Indian and Bengali villages, which this film [*Pather Panchali*] radiates eminently, makes it the truest possible approximation to the sweet emotional cobwebs of sorrow that Bibhutibhushan's *Saga of the Path* had woven to our inestimable delight.'
— *Amrita Bazar Patrika*, Calcutta, 9 September 1955

A Beautiful Picture, Fresh and Personal*

Lindsay Anderson

When Renoir made *The River* in Bengal, Ray was able to follow the shooting closely. That he learned much from this experience is obvious, yet he has made a film that is purely and deeply his own.

'To admire on principle,' Coleridge observed, 'is the only way to imitate without loss of originality.' Ray's admiration for Renoir is of this kind. Turning back indeed in an article which he contributed to *Sequence* in 1950 ('Renoir in Calcutta') I find him writing: 'To Renoir there is nothing more important in a film than the emotional integrity of the emotions it depicts. Technique is useful and necessary in so far as it contributes towards this integrity. Beyond that it is generally intrusive and exhibitionist.' And this is the quality of Ray's own film. Humbly, patiently, his camera reaches forward into life, exploring and exposing, with reverence and wonder.

Pather Panchali is adapted from a well-known Bengali novel (the title means, literally, 'Song of the Little Road'), but the translation into terms of cinema is complete. It is the story of a poor family living in a hopeless, patched-up hovel, in a small village. The father is a clerk, who dreams ineptly of being a poet; he is badly paid, and sometimes not paid at all. His wife has to make do from day to day with rice and a fruit and meat if they are lucky. There are two children, a girl and a boy, and an incredibly wizened capricious old lady whom they know as 'Auntie'. The lives of these people is the story of the film: there is no tight dramatic construction or conventional plot. The tension is poetic rather than dramatic, created by the artist's intimate contact with his material, physical as well as emotional. To make *Pather Panchali* Ray must have lived as closely with his characters as Flaherty had to live with his Polynesians, when he made *Moana*.

Everything is significant: small joys, bitterness and tragedies intermingled with the hard routine of every day. The mother prepares a meal, and the children play. Around the wretched house are shady woodland paths, stretches of water, fields of tall feathered grass. The children have no lack of delights and mysteries: the sweet-seller passing down the track, calling his wares, an express train charging powerfully across the plain, a performance by a troupe of strolling players. The film's rhythm is slow, absorbed, reflecting the rhythm of simple lives. There are too many mouths to feed, and the old lady, grown irritating beyond endurance, is turned away by the mother. She goes off to die alone in the forest – *Tobacco Road* shorn of its grotesque comedy. Insect life stirs the surface of the placid lake; the leaves of the water lilies flap in the rising wind; the rains begin. The little girl catches cold and becomes ill: rain beats into the hut, the threadbare hangings collapse, and there is nothing to protect the feverish little body. She dies. In the end, the rest of the family move away to the city. A snake glides slowly into the deserted home; father, mother and son sit patiently in the wagon. With this sad humanistic affirmation, resisting the rhetoric of a long shot, tenaciously holding his people's faces, Ray ends his film.

Pather Panchali is a beautiful picture, completely fresh and personal, which required great courage and perseverance to make. (Shooting was brought to a halt for a considerable period because money ran out.) It is to compliment Ray, not to deny his originality, that I mention names like Renoir and Flaherty. And another fertilizing influence has surely been the neo-realism of De Sica, Zavattini and Rossellini, with its equal rejection of dramatic conventions, and its passionate concern with the lives of the underprivileged.

* *Sight & Sound*, London, 1955

'... The most beautiful film indeed of all the films shown at the festival is the Indian film *Pather Panchali*. It makes me think of Romain Rolland's *Jean-Christophe* in the world of books and of Jean Renoir's *The River* in the world of films.'
— Andre Bazin in *Le Parisien libéré*

'... There are influences in his film [*Pather Panchali*] – Ray admits allegiance to Renoir and to the anti-dramatic principles of De Sica and Rossellini, but the influences were completely assimilated. ... In water, forest and plain, nature is a living presence. It is never easy to translate poetry, and words can barely convey the beauty and richness of the masterly film.'
— *The Times*, London, 19 May 1956

'... *Pather Panchali* is all the more remarkable because it is totally unlike the work of every other director in the teeming and affluent world of Indian film-making. ... The film is long and its pace is slow, but it does not seem slow. It is beautiful, poignant and severely true.'
— *Manchester Guardian*

'... Two principal recurrent images (are there) in *Pather Panchali*, the train and the pond. ... The pond is clearly associated with the past, old-age passivity, resignation in contrast to the children's carefree rush towards the future. But neither the train nor the pond is there just as a metaphysical trapping.'
— John Russell Taylor, *Directors & Directions*

'... The film is an experience rather than an entertainment ... The photography is in fine-drawn black and white. The pace is quite unhurried. ... Although small background sound is used with remarkable imagination, not the least charm of *Pather Panchali* is its blessed quiet.'
— C.A. Lejeune in *The Observer*, London

One of the Finest Films of the World*

Shouvik (Pankaj Dutta)

There's no need for us to be diffident and use qualifications such as 'perhaps', 'if' or 'but' any more. We now have good enough reasons to proclaim to the world unhesitatingly that we not only make more films than any other country, we are also capable of making films that can match the quality of the best-ever produced in the history of films in the world. We can say that with a great deal of pride after seeing *Pather Panchali*.

Pather Panchali is an outstanding literary creation of Bibhutibhushan Bandyopadhyay (Banerjee). Based on it, Satyajit Ray has, by sheer mastery of his screenplay and brilliant direction, created a cinematic work of such authentic originality that it is not possible to think of any other film ever exhibited in India, indigenous or foreign, that can be considered worthy of comparison with his *Pather Panchali*.

If you see the film and still have any doubts on this score, it will have to be attributed to a sense of humility in acknowledging the merits of home-grown products, or to haughty snobbishness, if not plain jealousy.

I have been watching films, local and foreign, for nearly twenty-five years now. I must have seen thousands of films over this period. Never before have I felt so thrilled, nor experienced so strong an urge to embellish my account of it with adjectives as I do now.

I do feel the time has arrived when we can shout to the whole world and claim that the all-round excellence of our films entitles them to be placed among the very best in the world. To think how this film was made makes me speechless in awe.

II

Satyajit Ray, who has written the screenplay of this film and also directed it, had not made any film before. Subrata Mitra, the cinematographer, had worked as an assistant cameraman in one film called *The River*. Bansi Chandragupta, the art director, was also relatively new in films. Their equipment, some of which had been sourced from discarded materials from abroad, were barely adequate for the task. And yet, like magicians, they have created a film that the best equipment of the world might not have managed.

Day after day, month after month, they worked with infinite patience to capture the essence of the original work, translate its mood and rhythm, record them on celluloid and then string them frame by frame into a superb cinematic expression. The patience, perseverance and toil that went into the making of the film are now part of history. It is a tale of how a dedicated and sensitive artist with a lively intellect has been able to

* First published in Bengali in *Desh* (influential Bengali literary weekly), 3 September 1955. Translated by Deepak Mukerjee.

Chunibala Devi as Indir Thakrun and Shampa 'Runki' Banerjee as little Durga

create a work of such impeccably luminous quality despite using dated equipment. As the leader of the team that made the film, Satyajit Ray succeeds in injecting so much life and vibrancy into every discipline of the art of film-making that we are able to see the end product in a completely new light as the film unfolds before our eyes. Never before have we seen a film like this where every unit leaves its unique mark on the end product, and yet collectively, they merge seamlessly into a homogeneous artistic confluence.

Bhupendra Ghosh and Satyen Chattopadhyay have worked on sound recording and sound mixing in several films before. But in *Pather Panchali*, the director lays out their work in such a way that we are able to appreciate their contribution in a new, wondrous light.

We have seen the use of music in films in so many ways. In this film, the music clearly bears the stamp of Pandit Ravi Shankar's genius. At the same time, Satyajit Ray demonstrates how music can be harnessed effectively to serve the needs of a film and add additional aesthetic value to it. His directorial genius not only shows us the importance of separate technical units of film-making performing their assigned roles, but also demonstrates how they can collectively lend grace and quality to the end product by working in symphonic unison with each other.

As we see instances of this magical transformation in scene after scene, we can hardly resist breaking out in spontaneous applause, 'Bravo, bravo!'

III

The originality of *Pather Panchali* is so startling that most commercially inclined minds would harbour doubts on the extent to which it can find a niche in the emotional space of filmgoers in our country. There are no songs in the film, no dance numbers, nor any levity bordering on the risqué. Naturally, no distributor came forward to help the makers with money to complete the film. Besides, virtually the entire team behind its making, including the actors, were new to cinema. The few who were not lacked sufficient box-office appeal. But Satyajit Ray was not prepared to compromise his dedication to cinema for money. The helping hand extended by the state of West Bengal and, particularly, by Dr Bidhan Chandra Roy, the chief minister of West Bengal, stands out against this background. In an unprecedented move that no maharaja of India had ever dared before, Dr Roy came forward to back the film with money from the state government coffers.

The world of cinema would certainly have been deprived of a great film had this help not come in. It is just as well that Satyajit Ray kept his part of the bargain by making sure that the state government's generosity paid off handsomely. As it turned out, the film has helped the state gain a reputation as a pioneer in promoting art and culture.

Every part of the film bears ample indications of the careful thought that has gone behind making it truly original and path-breaking. The film is replete with minute details and delicate little touches. Every one of them enchants our minds so subtly that it is impossible to do justice to them by trying to describe them. The humane appeal of the story also comes across so simply and naturally, and yet so overwhelmingly, that no human mind can possibly resist being profoundly moved by it. There is not a single detail in the film that is dispensable or unbecoming, nothing that fails to strike a poignant note in our minds and enchant us.

One can only admire and applaud all of this. It is almost unreal in its perfection, like a dream.

IV

Pather Panchali is a fairly bulky novel. It is a difficult and daring task to bring such a large work within the confines of a feature film of standard length. Besides, *Pather Panchali* is a descriptive tale of nature and of human emotions. It derives its main elements from bountiful nature and her abundant charms. Obviously, it is not possible to accommodate all of that in a film. Satyajit Ray has stayed well away from trying to do any such thing. And yet, its screenplay has not strayed an inch from the original.

That is an outstanding achievement. Satyajit Ray has successfully filtered out the essence from this bulky volume and portrayed its spirit so faithfully that there is no room at all for anyone who has seen it to feel disappointed.

Besides, I feel it is necessary to regard this film as an original creation in an artistic medium that stands well apart from literature. Admittedly, it is an adaptation of a work of literature. However, its translation into celluloid is so creative that it cries out for recognition as an original creation in cinema.

The storyline, after all, is simple. Harihar is an indigent Brahmin. When the film begins, his family consists of his wife Sarbajaya, daughter Durga, and his ageing cousin, Indir Thakrun. Sarbajaya is often at the receiving end of rebuke (by neighbours) because of naughty Durga's penchant for raiding their gardens in search of fruits. Sarbajaya takes her anger out on Indir Thakrun, of whom Durga is very fond. Sarbajaya's sharp temper has other sources as well. Harihar is out of work. Finances of the family are stretched.

When Indir Thakrun gets upset, she picks up her tattered wrapper and mat and her only other worldly possession, a brass tumbler, and leaves the house in a huff, muttering all sorts of discontent. Harihar writes plays in his spare time and dreams that the entire village will, one day, recognize his talent, ending all his sorrows.

Apu is born in this ambience – his dreamy eyes survey all that is around with limitless curiosity. Harihar lands himself a job. Indir Thakrun returns home. Days pass as Apu grows up. He runs around with his elder sister, but their aunt next door cannot stand them because of their poverty. Apu and Durga doze off while listening to Indir Thakrun's fairy tales. Apu gets into school. One day, while playing hide-and-seek with his sister, they see a passing train across the fields of white kaash flowers. New experiences enrich their lives.

Harihar's pay falls into arrears. Penury returns to the family. Harihar leaves for Bishnupur in search of work. There is no news from him for four months. Indir Thakrun, who had left, returns one afternoon. Sarbajaya's temper gets worse. Panting from her exertions as she returns, Indir Thakrun sits down in the shade and asks for a glass of water. Sarbajaya is having lunch. She sharply tells her that she had better get the water herself. Indir Thakrun comes near Sarbajaya to get some water and eyes Sarbajaya having lunch. She decides to leave the house again and departs with all her possessions.

On the way back home after playing in the village, Apu and Durga find their aunt sitting under a tree with her head tucked between her knees. They call her. She does not respond. And when they touch her, her body slumps to the earth in a heap. She is dead. Durga and Apu are scared.

Seasons change. The rains arrive, laden with clouds. Rainwater floods the village greens. Overjoyed, the siblings wade in water, romping in fun. Durga has fever when they return home. A kindly neighbour gets a doctor to see her. It is pneumonia.

Durga dies on a stormy, rain-spattered night. Harihar returns a few days later. He has brought money. Sarbajaya's repressed grief explodes in uncontrollable sobs just as Harihar hands over to her a sari he has brought for Durga. Harihar decides to leave the village and departs for Varanasi with his wife and son.

V

There is nothing at all very dramatic in the story to enthral the audience. All that it has is a carefully designed unfolding of a story set in an ambience that readily resonates with our emotions. Each episode in the film is built from elements taken from trifling little vignettes of life. There is nothing that is unrealistic, nor anything that does not ring true in this beautifully poignant tale of a life of endless struggle.

The story is about Durga and Apu. They are born in unrelieved poverty. In a way, they are nature's own children. Indir Thakrun, their ageing aunt, is the haven of loving assurance. It is in this milieu that they find another aunt, a next-door neighbour, pour scorn on them and their family for no reason other than their poverty. Her children, however, are different. They are keen to play with them and befriend them, but their mother's forbidding supervision keeps them apart.

> 'The first film [*Pather Panchali*] by the masterly Satyajit Ray – possibly the most unembarrassed and natural of directors – is a quiet reverie about the life of an impoverished Brahmin family in a Bengal village. Beautiful, sometimes funny, and full of love, it brought a new vision of India to the screen.'
> **— Pauline Kael, influential American film critic**

They also find help arriving unsolicited from another lady, a kind neighbour, when they are starving and have nothing at all to eat. Nobody else in the village shows the slightest concern for their well-being. And yet, when Durga passes away, and the family decides to leave for Varanasi for good, the same neighbours are full of gratuitous advice on why they should not leave their home and hearth!

They see the village pandit, a cane in one hand, teaching children and selling goods from his store at the same time. While all this is going on, Chakrabarti drops in, helps himself generously to some hair oil from the shop and promptly uses it on his hair. And then, as an afterthought as he prepares to leave, he promises to commute the pandit's annual dues to a community event in exchange for the oil!

Sarbajaya's heartless treatment of her destitute sister-in-law, the ageing Indir Thakrun, bred no doubt of her frustration at her inability to raise her children properly, uncovers another dimension of the human mind.

Can we imagine a better cinematic expression of the dreams and hopes of a young village girl than the drop of tear we see welling up in the corner of Durga's eyes as she watches her playmate being dressed up for her wedding?

Tiny and trifling these details may be, they are laden with rich emotional content. There is nothing in the film that does not leave a lasting impression on our minds.

VI

There are lots of small bits and pieces that are noticeable in the design of the film. Consider the scene where Durga steals tamarind. Quietly, she asks Apu to get her some oil. She then makes a pickle out of it and puts it in her mouth, and then in Apu's. The scene is so composed that most viewers will find their mouths watering as they watch the scene. This is the stuff that this film is made of – events that are commonplace, unadorned and natural, and yet so evocative that they resonate readily with the viewers' memory and their finer sensibilities.

Consider another scene where Durga and Apu play hide-and-seek among the white kaash flowers. Suddenly, they notice a telegraph pole and stop. They put their ear to the pole and are struck with wonder when they hear a humming sound. Then they hear the shrill whistle of a train engine and start running after the train. And so do the viewers, who experience the same emotions!

A deep sense of tranquillity envelops our minds as we see the children in the film following the vendor of sweets, their feet in step with the beat of the bells on the vendor's ankles, and the rhythmic swinging of earthen pots laden with sweets, or when we see a picnic fizzling out because of a tiff over someone forgetting to bring salt, and other such simple incidents.

And then there is that scene of pomp where a band strikes up celebratory notes at the wedding of the daughter of a neighbour. Or the sombre scene of Apu's birth that precedes it.

Indir Thakrun's habit of walking away from home every so often and then returning strikes a melancholy note, just as the scene where she is found dead with her head slumped on her knees, and her stiff body collapsing like a heap the moment Durga nudges her, makes us profoundly sorry.

I do not think death has ever been portrayed in this manner in films.

Another memorably poignant scene is where Indir Thakrun tells fairy tales to her niece and nephew in the evening. When they fall asleep, she leans on a wall and sings, '*Hari din toh gelo sandhya holo, paar karo amaare*'. The piteous earnestness of her appeal to God to help her depart from this world is deeply moving.

Apu's innocent eyes, as full of curiosity when he watches a sword fight in a village play as when he watches her dear aunt's lifeless body fall in a heap, follow the viewer everywhere and haunt him.

Who can forget the ineffably beautiful dramatic impact of the scene where Apu, while packing up his books in preparation for the family's departure to Varanasi, discovers a string of beads her sister had hidden inside a jar made of a broken coconut shell atop a shelf. We know, of course,

that this string of beads belonged to a girl next door. Accused of theft, Durga had denied the charge but was beaten severely by her mother. The expression on Apu's face tells us how heavily the memory still weighs on his mind as we see him chuck it into the depths of a pond.

Incomparable are the scenes of the monsoon rains in the film. Cloud upon cloud gathers on the sky. We hear a storm brewing and see Apu and Durga run and run. Frogs are out swimming in pools of water. A single drop of rainwater falls on the bald pate of an angler with a fishing rod. The gentle patter of raindrops on lotus leaves soon turns to a crescendo as the whole sky explodes in rains. The sight of Durga getting drenched in the rain with her hair let loose – what an incredibly evocative scene!

Consider another scene on the fateful night when howling winds and driving rain herald Durga's death. The jute curtain on the window swings wildly, as if it would be blown away any moment. The door fastener rattles precariously. Sarbajaya is with the ailing Durga snuggling up to her lap, and Apu is reclining beside Durga. Amid all this turbulence, Sarbajaya's never-say-die resolve to fight for survival shines through her deeply anxious face, informing the scene with a wonderfully dramatic quality. Her predicament evokes a ready resonance in the minds of the audience the like of which has never been seen in cinema before.

Glimpses of the slush the morning after, of roofs blown away and of dead frogs, heighten the poignancy of the scene. And then comes the climax. We see Harihar return home after a long tour. He hands over to Sarbajaya a sari he has brought as a present for Durga. It is not possible for any viewer not to be overcome by the pathos of the scene as Sarbajaya's suppressed scream of despair rends his heart.

VII

The elements used in creating this milieu are such that they lend a universal appeal to the drama – an appeal that will deeply touch any mind anywhere, across borders and class barriers, be they rich or poor, educated or unlettered, Indian or foreign.

You could, if you like, call the design of the film neo-realism, a style of film-making introduced in post-war Italy by De Sica and others. But Satyajit Ray has surpassed them all and taken the art of film-making to a level where he has no peer.

By presenting harsh reality in rich lyrical terms, Satyajit Ray succeeds in imparting to his work an emotional momentum that unfolds ever so gently, like a poem, on the sensibilities of the audience, and makes them realize anew the greatness of the art of cinema.

Everything in this film is harmonious. The actors look like the characters they are playing. Watching Subir Banerjee as Apu or Uma Dasgupta as Durga, it is impossible to imagine any other face that would fit these two roles. Nor is it possible to think that they could walk and behave in any other way than what we see them do in the film.

Chunibala Devi as Indir Thakrun is simply amazing. She is about ninety. Her skin has become loose and crumpled with age as have her facial features. And yet she produces a brilliantly sensitive performance. It is an incredible feat for someone who may well be the senior-most actress in the world. No wonder, the scene of her death in the film disturbs us so much.

Kanu Banerjee, as the impoverished Brahmin and the ever optimistic village playwright, looks exactly his part. We just cannot think of any other person in that role. And so is Karuna Banerjee as Sarbajaya in the role of the hapless wife doomed to a life of deprivation, but yet uncomplaining. She may not be able to feed her children well, but no one can fault her indomitable spirit. Intensely self-respecting, she would rather go stealthily at dawn to pawn her utensils than ask for help even from the most generous of her neighbours. Karuna Banerjee's acting vividly brings out this typically Indian trait of suffering in silence.

In the end, Harihar shows up after a long time with a sari for Durga. Overcome with grief for Durga, Sarbajaya breaks down. Karuna Banerjee's poignant portrayal of Sarbajaya's emotional explosion elevates this tragic scene to levels of artistic excellence rarely seen.

Every minor character has also been chosen to ensure that the persons fit the roles perfectly. We discover a completely new Tulsi Chakrabarti when we see him multitasking as a grocery store manager-cum-schoolteacher.

How can we forget the candy seller's dancing gait as his sharp eyes survey young buyers? No matter how small the role is, the choice of every actor in this film is unerringly appropriate. One feels as if no other selection would have done justice to the roles.

VIII

Subrata Mitra's photography adds to the neo-realist narrative style followed in the making of this film. It is his debut but he produces work of the highest standard. He succeeds in imbuing an eloquent dramatic intensity to scenes of nature where no words are spoken.

The film has been shot in a village called Boral, not very far from Kolkata. There are very few sequences in it that were filmed under artificial lights of a studio; the bulk of the film was shot outdoors in the natural light of the village. Perhaps that is what makes every frame of the film vibrate with life. This is evident in any of the following scenes: Apu and Durga frolicking in the bamboo groves; dense white kaash flowers undulating in waves in the wind; the candy seller prancing along the village pond with kids in tow; frogs swimming in water before it starts to rain; dragonflies hovering over kalmi stalks; a metal pitcher that belonged to the dead Indir Thakrun rolling down to the pond while a fly settles on her corpse; a dog shaking off rainwater from its back; a cortege on rustic roads; rains on lotus leaves followed by scenes of downpour, and so many other scenes! Every inch of the film is marked by excellent photography. Every frame in it brims with startling novelty that leaves one in no doubt of its originality. As far as technique is concerned, the scenes of Durga getting wet in the rains and of the turbulence of the night when Durga dies have to be hailed as unforgettable cinematic achievements.

Karuna Banerjee as Sarbajaya and Kanu Banerjee as Harihar

Like the camera, the role of sound in the film is equally imaginative. The sound of the approaching railway train, for example, echoing on the vibrating telegraph pole, or, of the howling storm on a rainy night, the swish of white kaash flowers swaying in the wind – all these sounds are worth careful attention. Bhupen Ghosh and Satyen Chattopadhyay scale rare heights in sound recording and sound mixing in this film.

Art direction and music too achieve levels of excellence in this film that are sensational. Every scene – whether it is Harihar's home, the schoolmaster's store or the wedding – is so laid out that it replicates reality meticulously. There is not an iota of artifice in Bansi Chandragupta's art direction just as there is no trace of artifice in the background musical score composed by Ravi Shankar. Shankar relies on indigenous musical instruments and uses simple, rustic tunes that add an enchanting allure to the film. However, when the need arises to communicate the fury of nature, he does not flinch from doing so. From this point of view, Ravi Shankar's music in the film reaches unsurpassable heights. There is great novelty in the way he has used a variety of instruments to produce a harmonious whole. Dulal Dutta's editing skills are also praiseworthy.

IX

It is impossible to list in words all the virtues of *Pather Panchali*. I do not think we have ever seen a film that is so perfect in so many ways. It is a film that has the power to command total attention of the audience every moment of its duration and hold them spellbound. To appreciate the glory of a garden, one does not need every flower pointed out separately and its beauty explained. *Pather Panchali*'s virtues too will, by themselves, keep audiences enthralled.

'... [*Pather Panchali* is] one of the most stunning first films in movie history. Ray is a welcome jolt of flesh, blood and spirit.'
— Jack Kroll in *Newsweek*

'[*Pather Panchali* is] as deeply beautiful and plainly poetic as any movie ever made. Rare and exquisite.'
— Hazel-Dawn Dumpert, *Los Angeles Weekly*

'[*Pather Panchali* is] one of the greatest pictures ever made.'
— Philip French in *The Observer, London*

'It was the birth of a cinema, certainly the birth of a new kind of Indian cinema. ... Certainly director Satyajit Ray and cinematographer Subrata Mitra showed a miraculous gift for lighting scenes, coaxing intimate and utterly convincing performances from children and other non-professional actors, and allowing narrative to grow seamlessly.'
— Stuart Jeffries in *The Guardian, London*

In the Beginning There Was *Pather Panchali**

Adoor Gopalakrishnan

In recent years, I have been asked more than once to list the all-time greats of my choice in cinema. I have every time found it next to impossible to limit my 'bests' to ten. In some of my lists, new choices replaced earlier ones. In this not-so-easy exercise, remarkably and justifiably, one film was constantly topping the list: Satyajit Ray's *Pather Panchali.*

Pather Panchali, for me, marks the beginning of the true Indian cinema – a beginning for all of us. It was not only a total negation of the soulless and superficial all-India cinema indifferent to real people and issues, but also an affirmation of the emergence of the first consummate artist on the subcontinent's motion picture scene. So, for us all – ardent lovers of this dynamic medium of art – in the beginning there was ... *Pather Panchali.*

And then there was the regional cinema coming to the fore, asserting its rightful place on the national scene with genuine cinematic expressions mirroring meaningfully the motions of everyday life as lived and experienced by common people.

The kind neighbour, Nilmani's wife (Aparna Devi), comforts Sarbajaya (Karuna Banerjee) in a poignant still from *Pather Panchali*

Pather Panchali made a total departure in the course of our cinema in that Indian cinema can be seen and studied now only in two major divisions: the Indian cinema before *Pather Panchali* and the Indian cinema after *Pather Panchali.* This one film, for the first time, for all Indians to note, asserted in no unequivocal terms that cinema was an art and it could not any longer be relegated to a corner as a sheer vehicle of 'entertainment'. It suddenly widened the scope of cinema. Its practitioners came to assume a higher status. Indian cinema, in the true sense of the term, slowly started to gain confidence.

It was those novel and uncompromising works of Ray and his peers, most importantly Ritwik Ghatak and Mrinal Sen, that instilled a certain courage and spirit in the aspiring film-makers who were to make an impact in their respective regions in the decades that followed.

Ray's influence on the film-makers of the present generation is simply undeniable; even those who haven't been fortunate to study his works formally in an academic institution have managed to get access to them at special festivals and society screenings. His films became the hallmark of quality in our cinema. And no serious practitioner of the medium could afford to ignore them. They came to be looked upon as the models of accomplishment in film art. Thus virtually made into a reference of quality, every film of note from other film-makers tended to be scrutinized and assessed

* First published in *Satyajit Ray: An Intimate Master*, edited by Santi Das, Kolkata: Allied Publishers, 1998. **Adoor Gopalakrishnan** is one of India's most well-known film-makers and a stalwart of the New Indian Cinema.

as either 'as good as' or 'not as good as' or very often 'nowhere near' Ray.

While historically there is no denying that *Pather Panchali* was Ray's best, the film that moves me most deeply every time I watch it, is *Aparajito.* I cannot help tears welling up in my eyes as I watch with profound empathy the relationship between the mother and the son unfolding in a saga of pain, isolation, love, longing and death.

I have my favourites even amongst Ray's so-called minor films. We have nothing in our cinema which can be compared with the sweetness and charm of those films Ray made for teenagers. *Sonar Kella, Joy Baba Felunath, Goopi Gyne Bagha Byne, Hirak Rajar Deshe* – all vibrate with wit and wisdom, magic and mystery, and imagination and adventure no child or adult can ever resist to be enthralled by. They are meant for children of all ages who have not lost their innocence.

> '"I can never forget the excitement in my mind after seeing it," Akira Kurosawa said about Satyajit Ray's first film, *Pather Panchali,* and it's true, this movie, made from next to nothing, mostly with untrained actors, by a director who was learning (and making up) the rules as he went along, is a work of such lyrical and emotional force that it becomes, for its audiences, as potent as their most deeply personal memories.' — **Salman Rushdie**

Ray's last films, *Ganashatru, Shakha-Prashakha* and *Agantuk* (here let me take the liberty to group them together as the 'moral trilogy'), were reflective of his anxious concern at the erosion of values fast eating into the vitals of the society. The artist who came on the scene saluting life with the sad and sweet saga of Apu in a historic trilogy was bidding goodbye to his audience with a pang of pain in his heart. The society, as seen, lived in and portrayed in these films is a degenerate one; it has come a long way from the quiet and dignified life of the pristine past.

The 'city stories', *Mahanagar, Pratidwandi* and *Seemabaddha*, legitimately belong to the present. They talk about the incompatibility of old values with the practicable attitudes and postures in a changing world visibly different and indifferent to finer sensitivities.

Jalsaghar, Devi, Charulata, Shatranj Ke Khiladi, Ghare Baire and *Sadgati* – the period films – exude the grandeur and gentility of a time past: romantic, nostalgic yet inevitably bound to change and transform.

Aranyer Din Ratri and *Kanchenjungha* take the characters away from their natural moorings – the wilderness of the city – and place them against unfamiliar settings – the bountiful elemental nature – weaving chiaroscuros of human passion, foibles and penitence.

There are of course quite a few other films, like *Abhijan, Chiriyakhana* and more importantly, *Ashani Sanket*, which defy easy categorization and analysis. All the same, there is no Ray film, short or minor, which would not impart the viewer the joy of unmitigated aesthetic experience.

For me, watching a Ray film is always revealing and rewarding, no matter how many times I have seen it before. Come to think of it, of how many world masters can one say this?

A sketch from *Aam Aantir Bhenpu*

'I am reminded of the scene – Apu and Durga rushing through the kaash fields to catch a glimpse of the train. Impeccable! Or the musical gait of the sweetmeat vendor ... Incredible! I especially liked Durga's death scene, the heightened melodrama that informs Kanu Banerjee's performance in this scene backed by the wail of the taarsaanai in lieu of Karuna Banerjee actually crying. Equally memorable is the appropriate use of the theme music on the enchanting strains of the flute ... it plays in your memory long after the film ends. It is as if the theme music is the life of the film.'

– Ritwik Ghatak

(translated from the Bengali by Shantanu Ray Chaudhuri)

'He started shooting his first film (a masterpiece) in 1952 at age thirty-one. He finished his last (twenty-nine films later) in 1991 at age seventy. One of the central film-makers of the twentieth century, one of the great story-inventors and tellers in his or any country, one of the most moving and inspiring voices in the history of the cinema: Satyajit Ray (director, scenarist, composer, novelist, illustrator), remains, for me, the ideal – and the definition of the word "artist".'

– **Wes Anderson**

THE SKETCHBOOK

PAGE 1

PAGE 2

PAGE 3

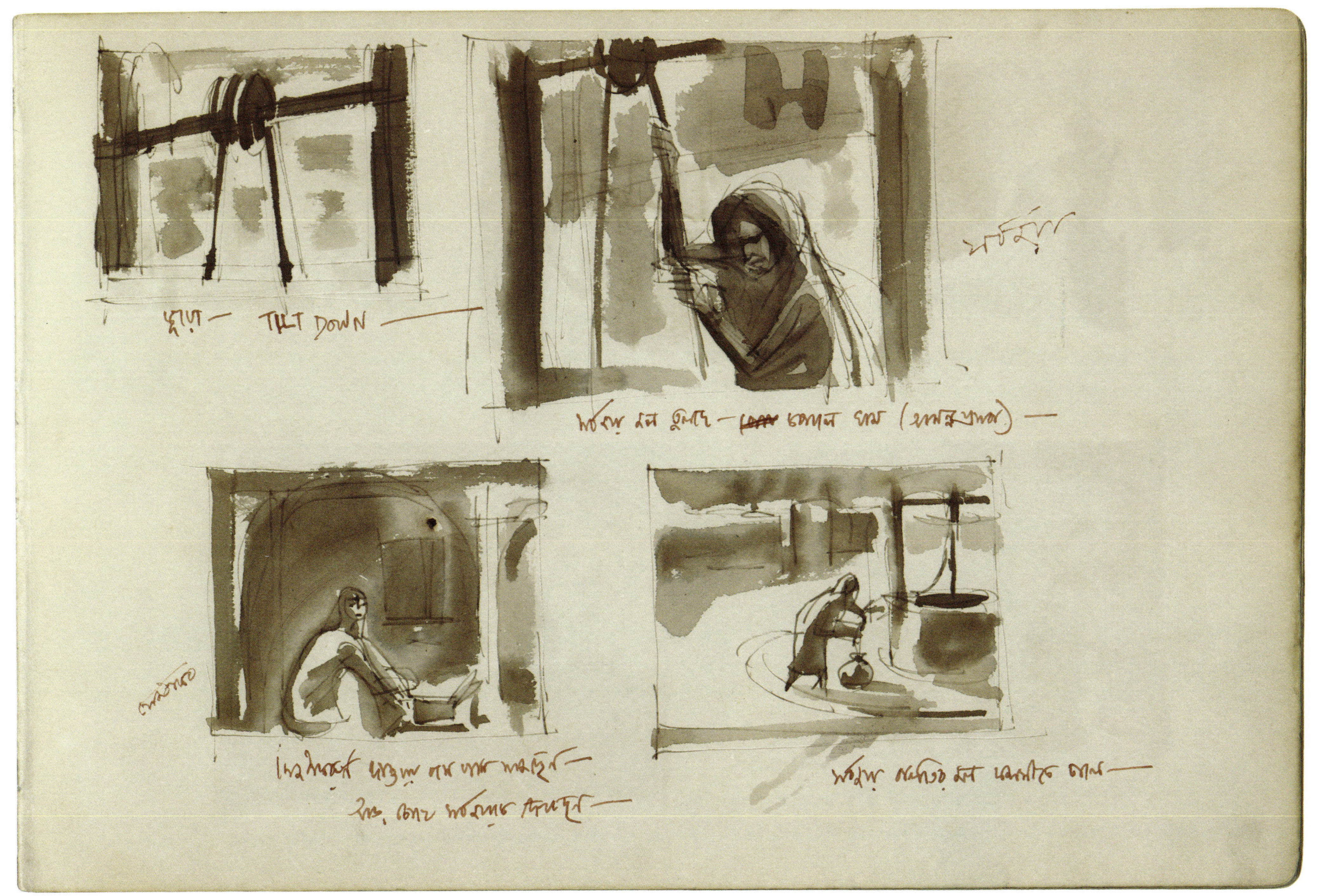

PAGE 4

PAGE 5

PAGE 6

PAGE 7

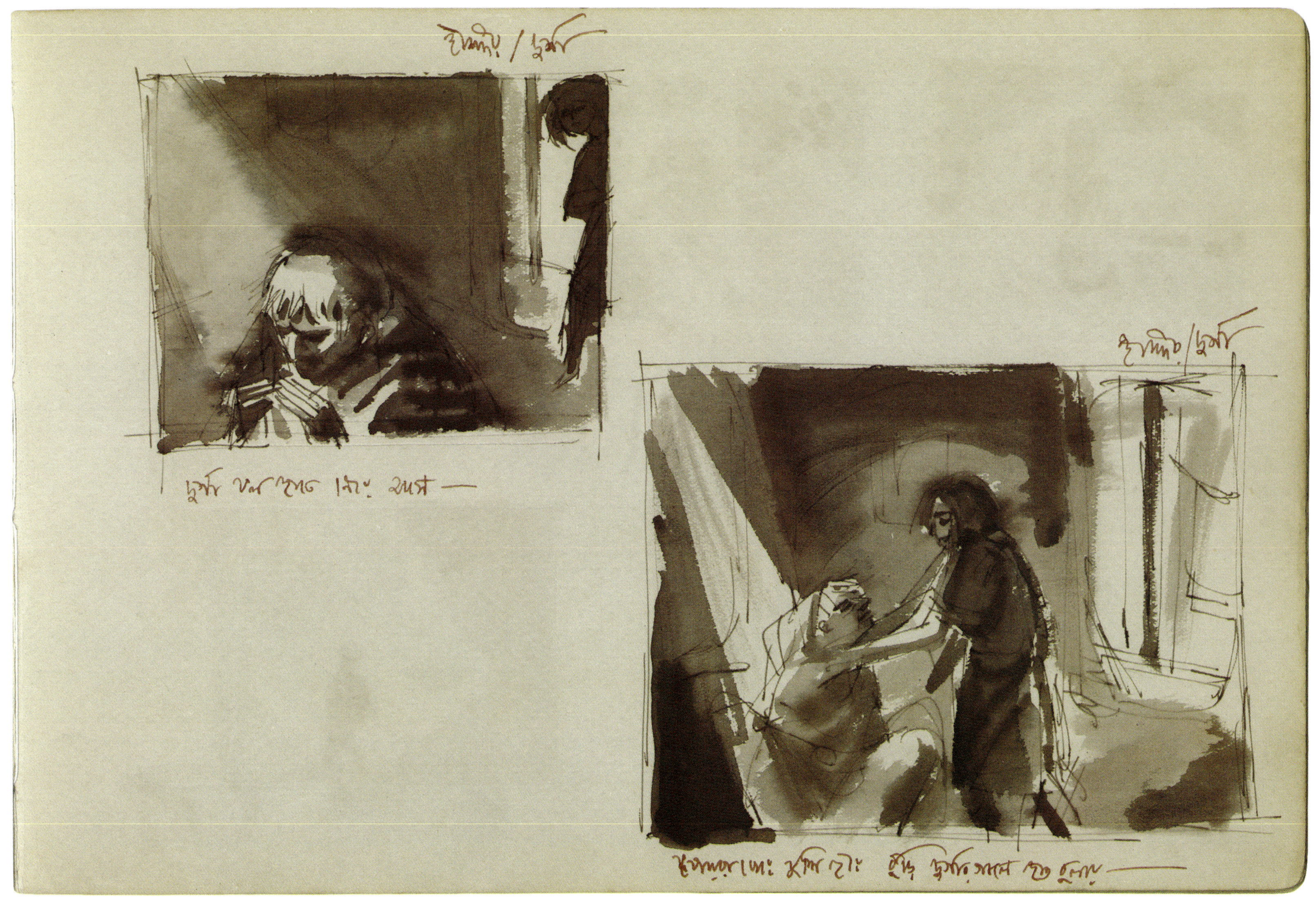

PAGE 8

PAGE 9

PAGE 10

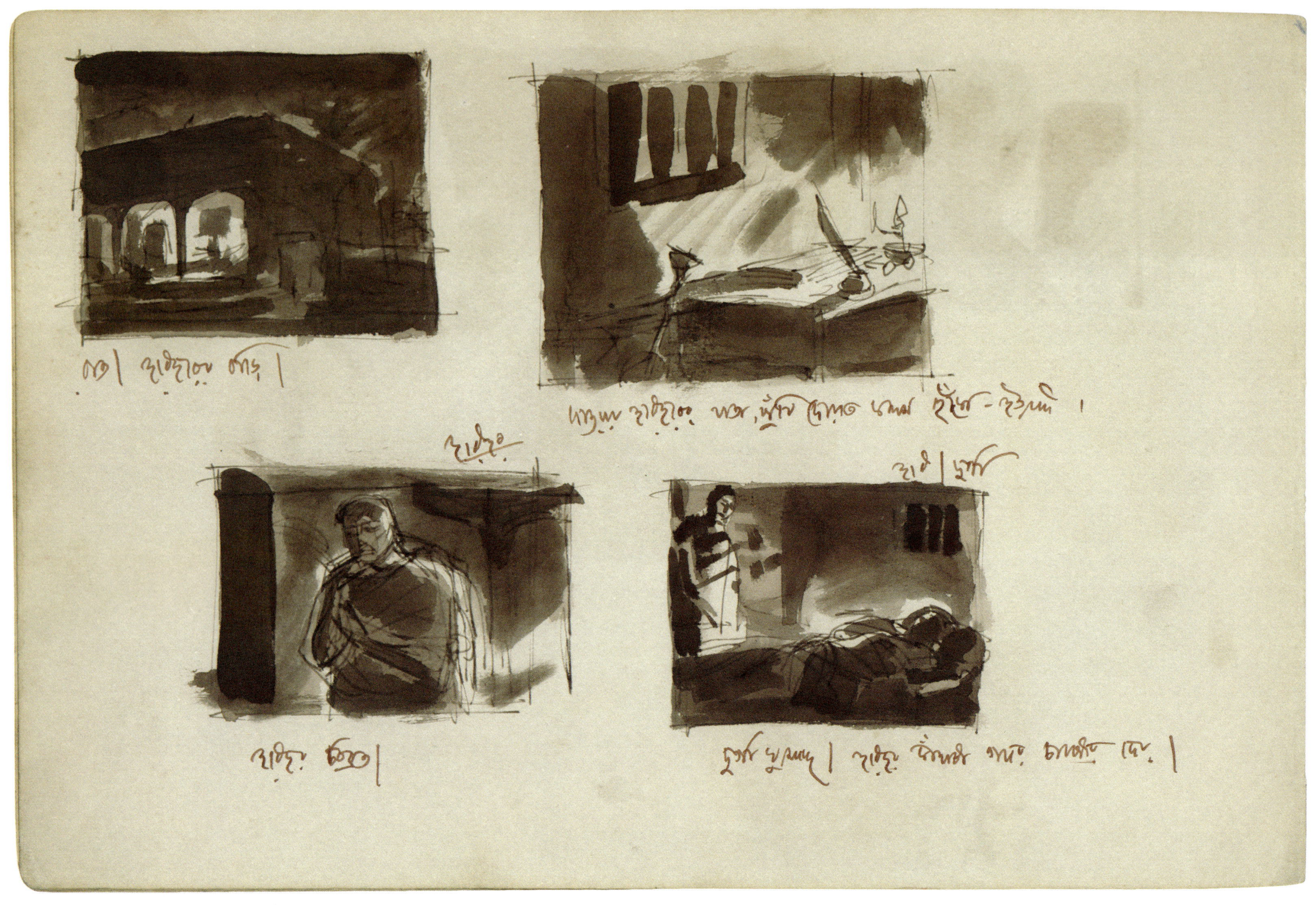

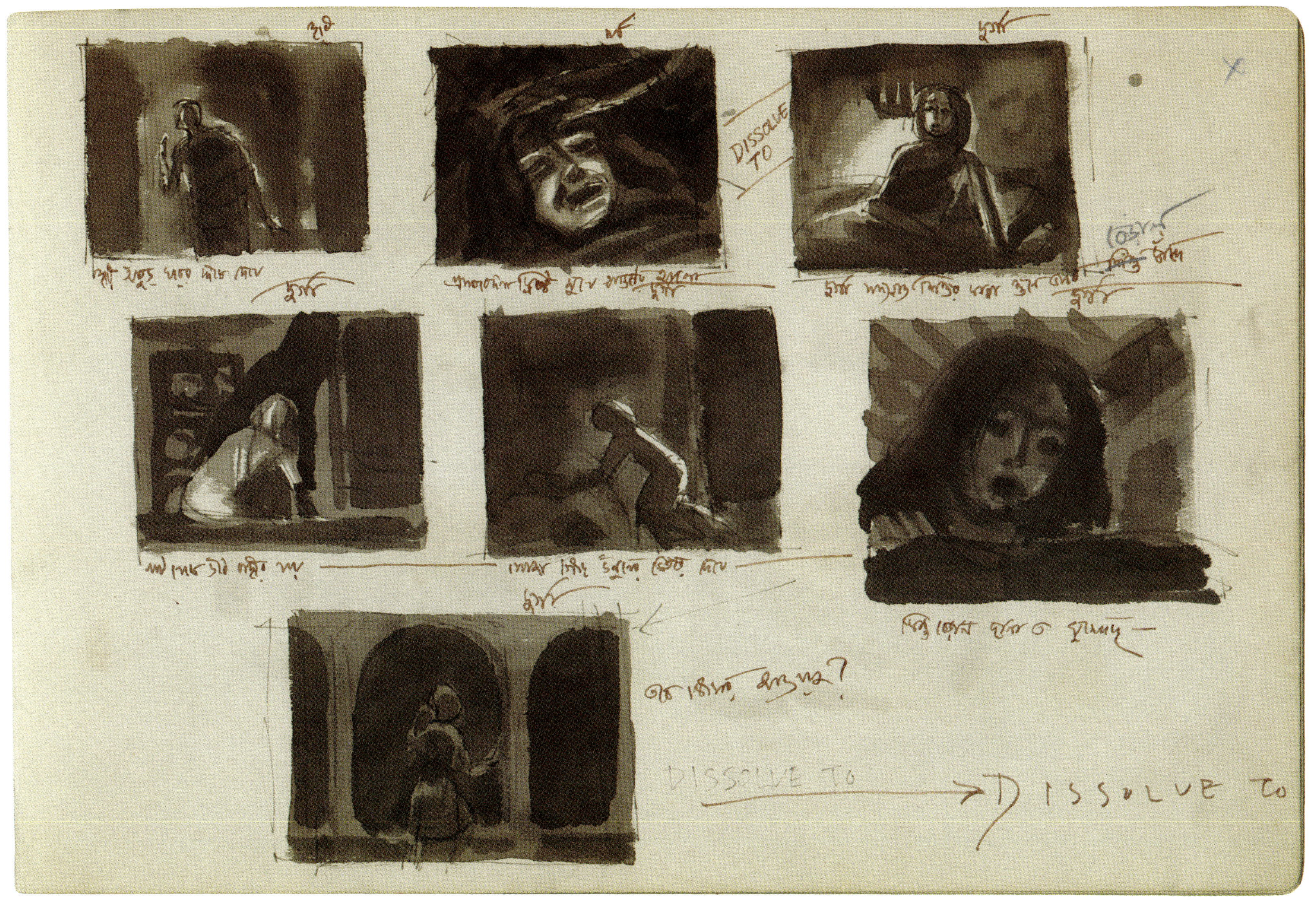

PAGE 12

PAGE 13

PAGE 14

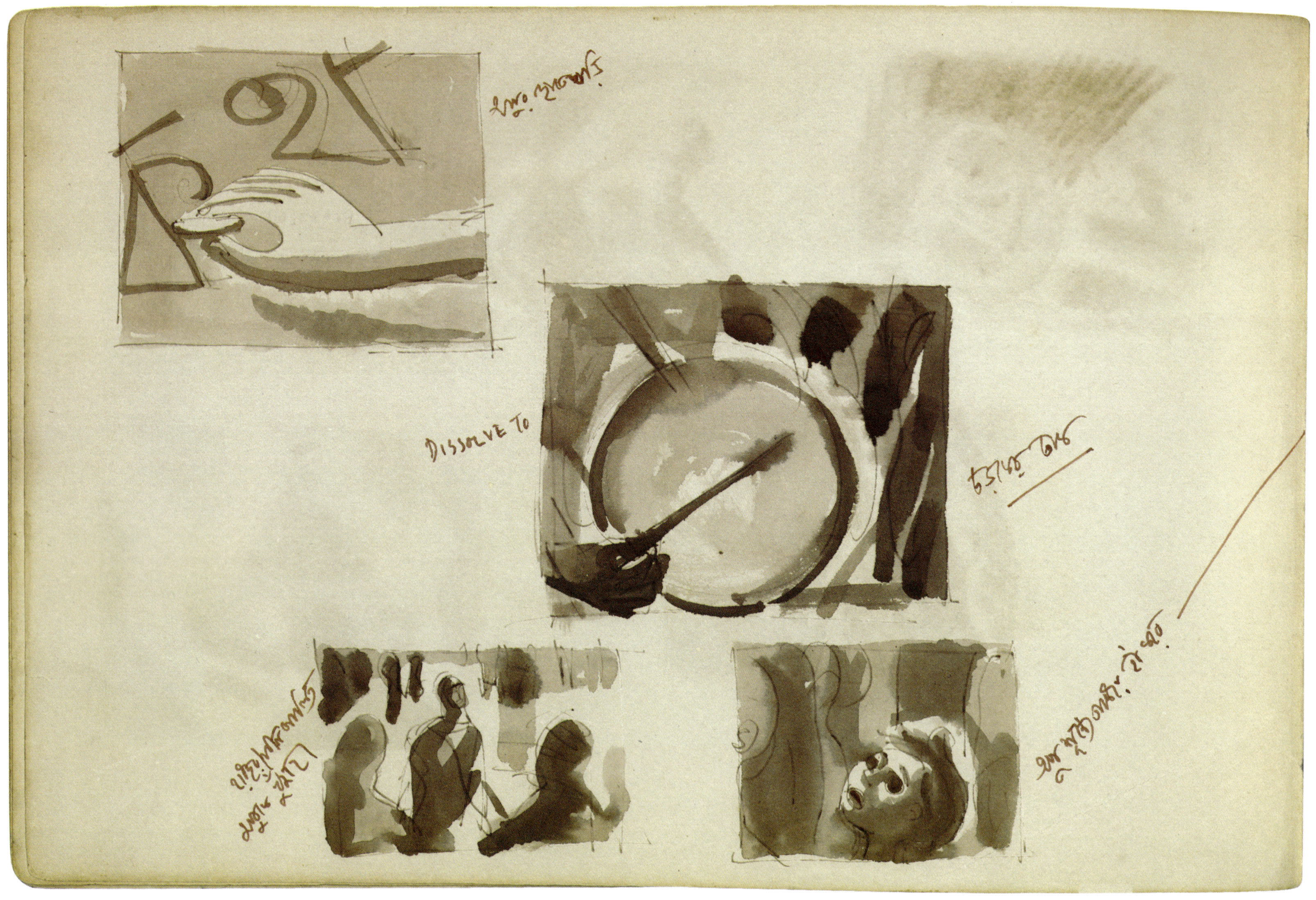

PAGE 15

PAGE 16

PAGE 17

PAGE 18

PAGE 19

PAGE 20

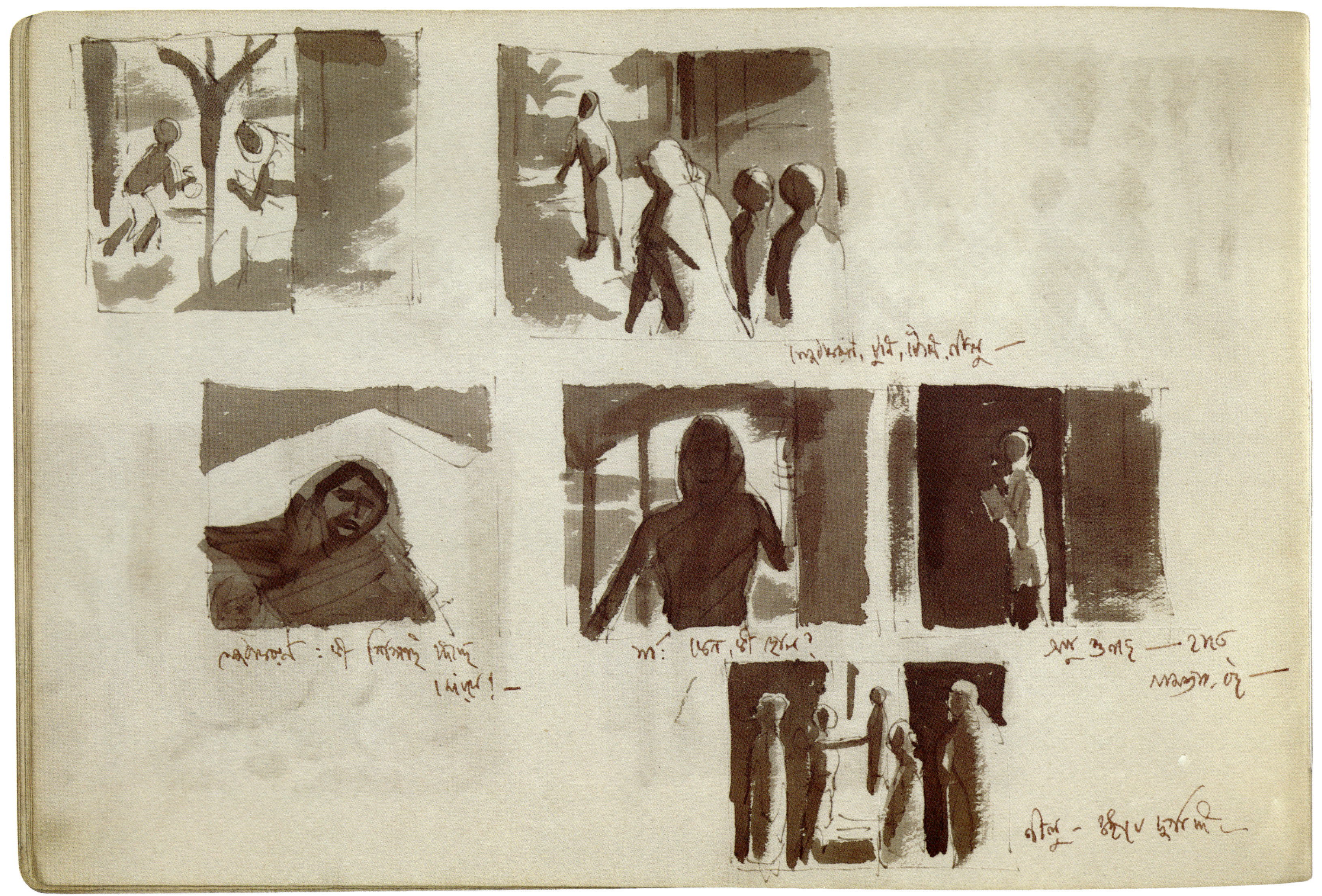

PAGE 21

PAGE 22

PAGE 23

PAGE 24

PAGE 25

PAGE 26

PAGE 27

PAGE 28

PAGE 29

PAGE 30

PAGE 31

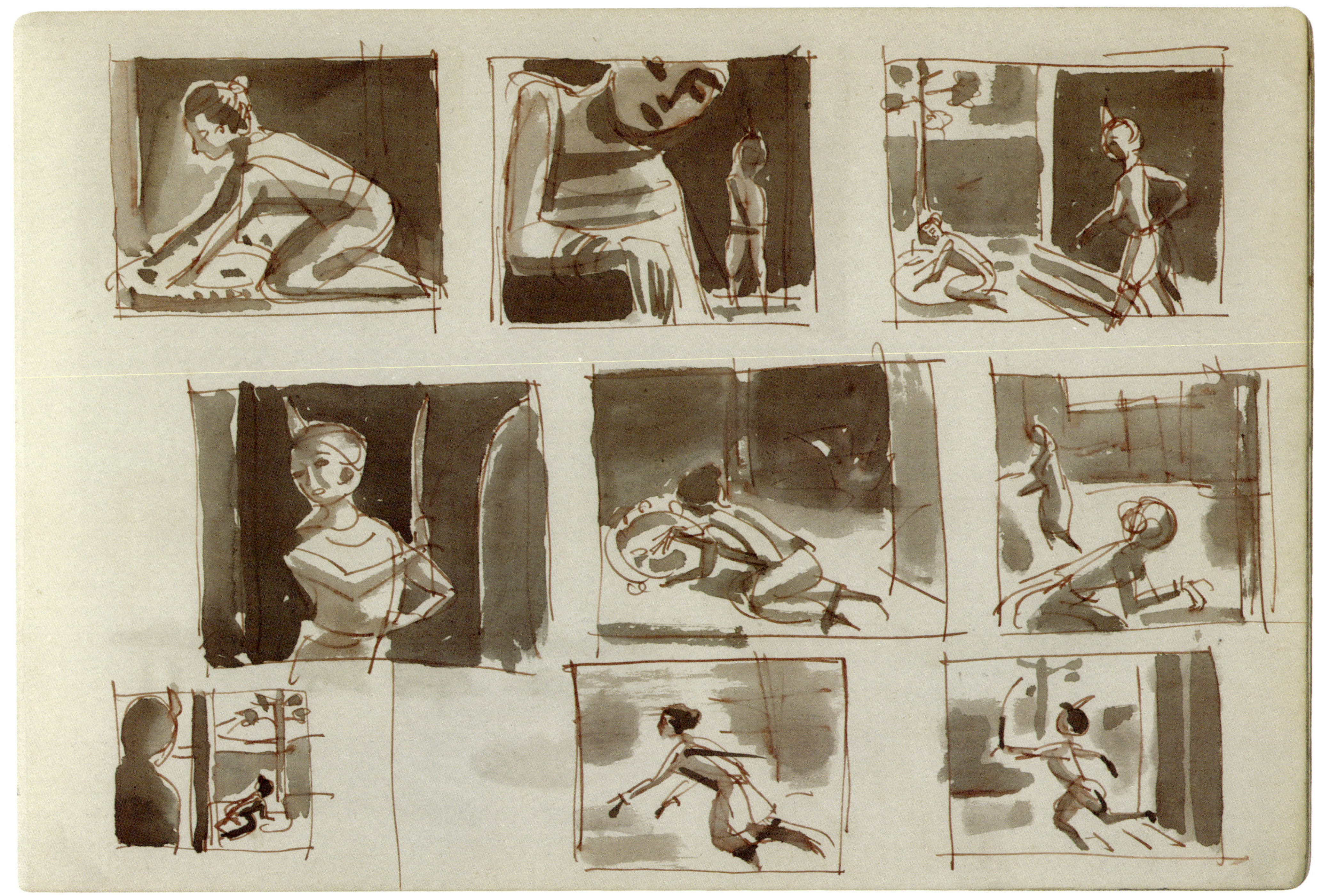

PAGE 32

PAGE 33

PAGE 34

PAGE 35

PAGE 36

PAGE 37

PAGE 38

PAGE 39

PAGE 40

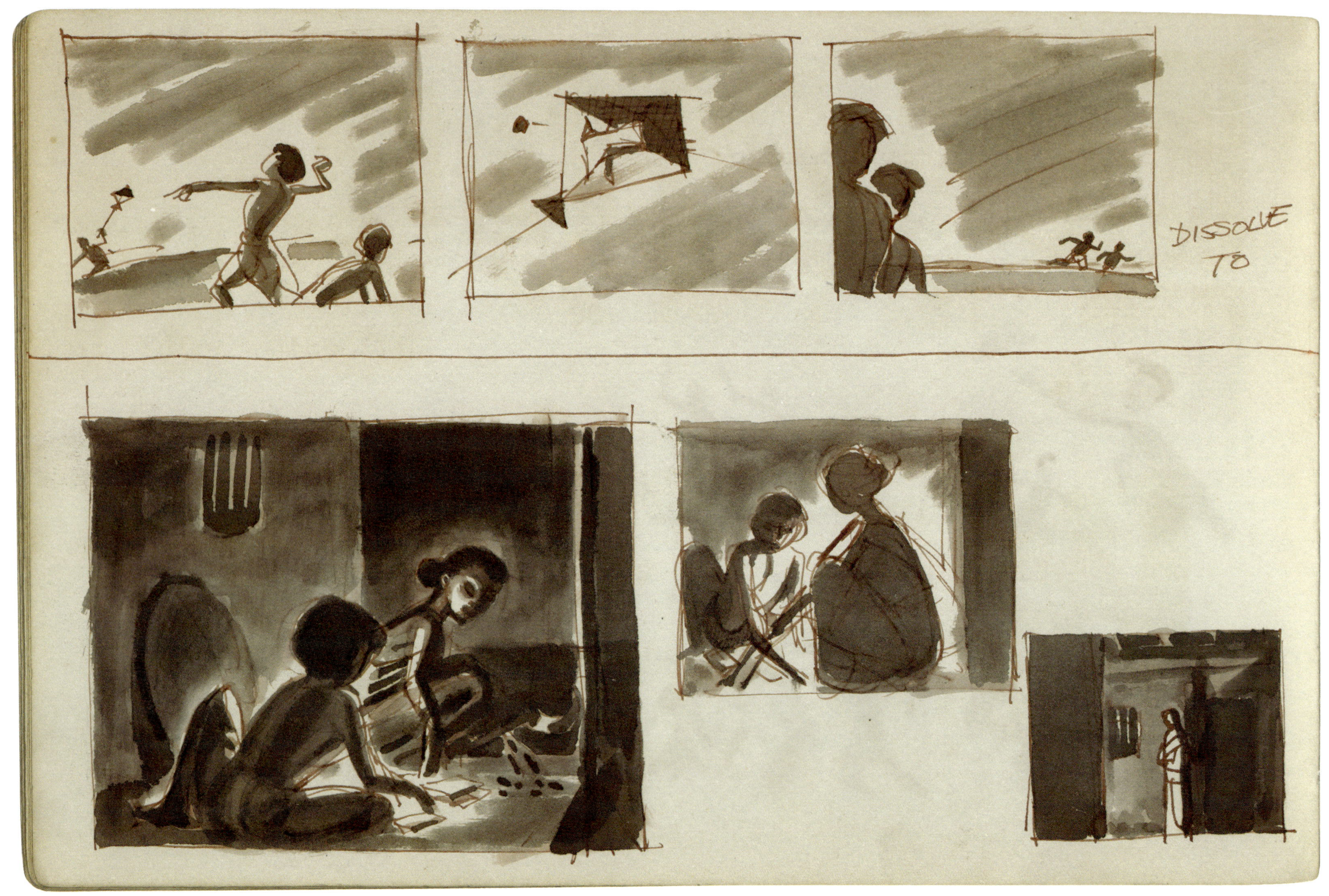

PAGE 41

PAGE 42

PAGE 43

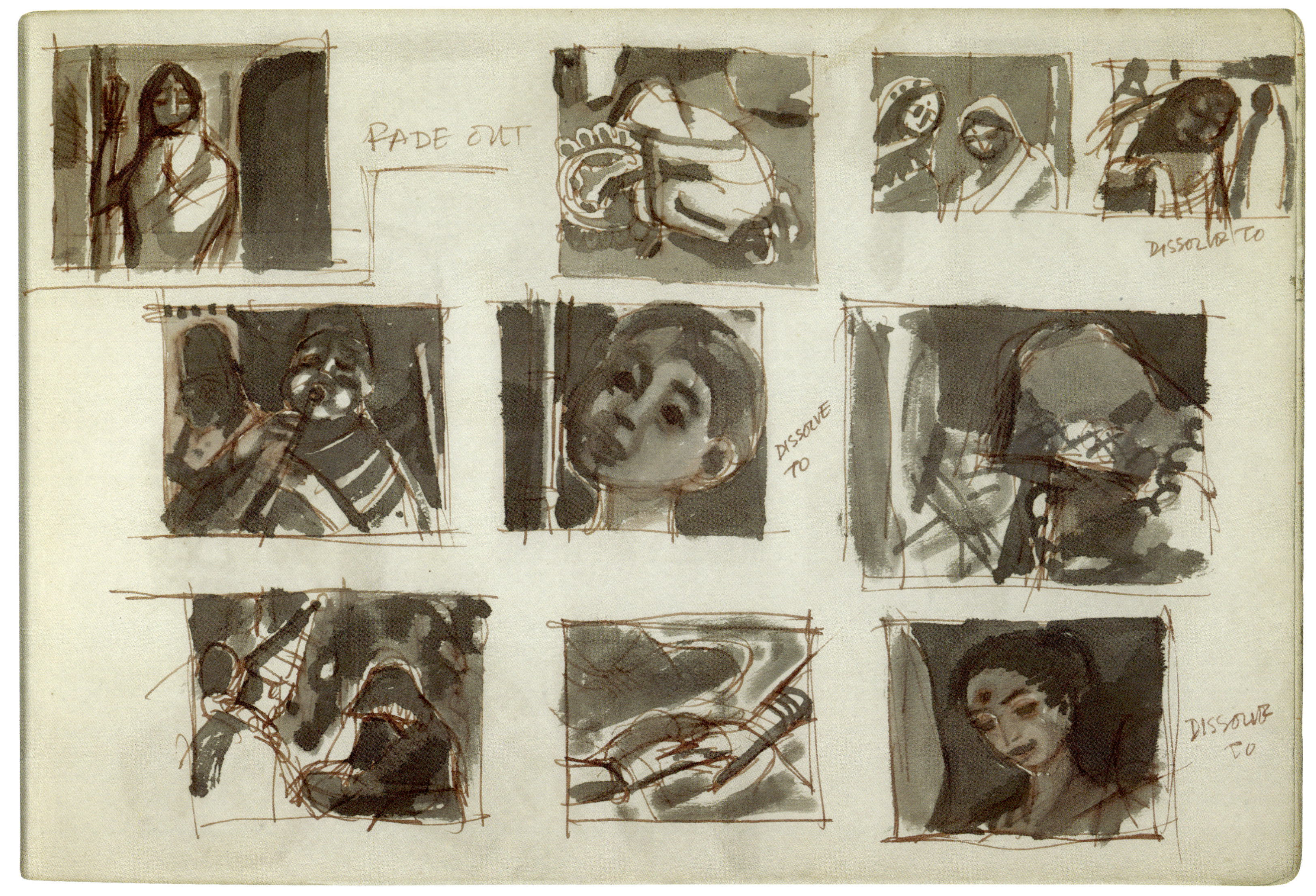

PAGE 44

PAGE 45

PAGE 46

PAGE 47

PAGE 48

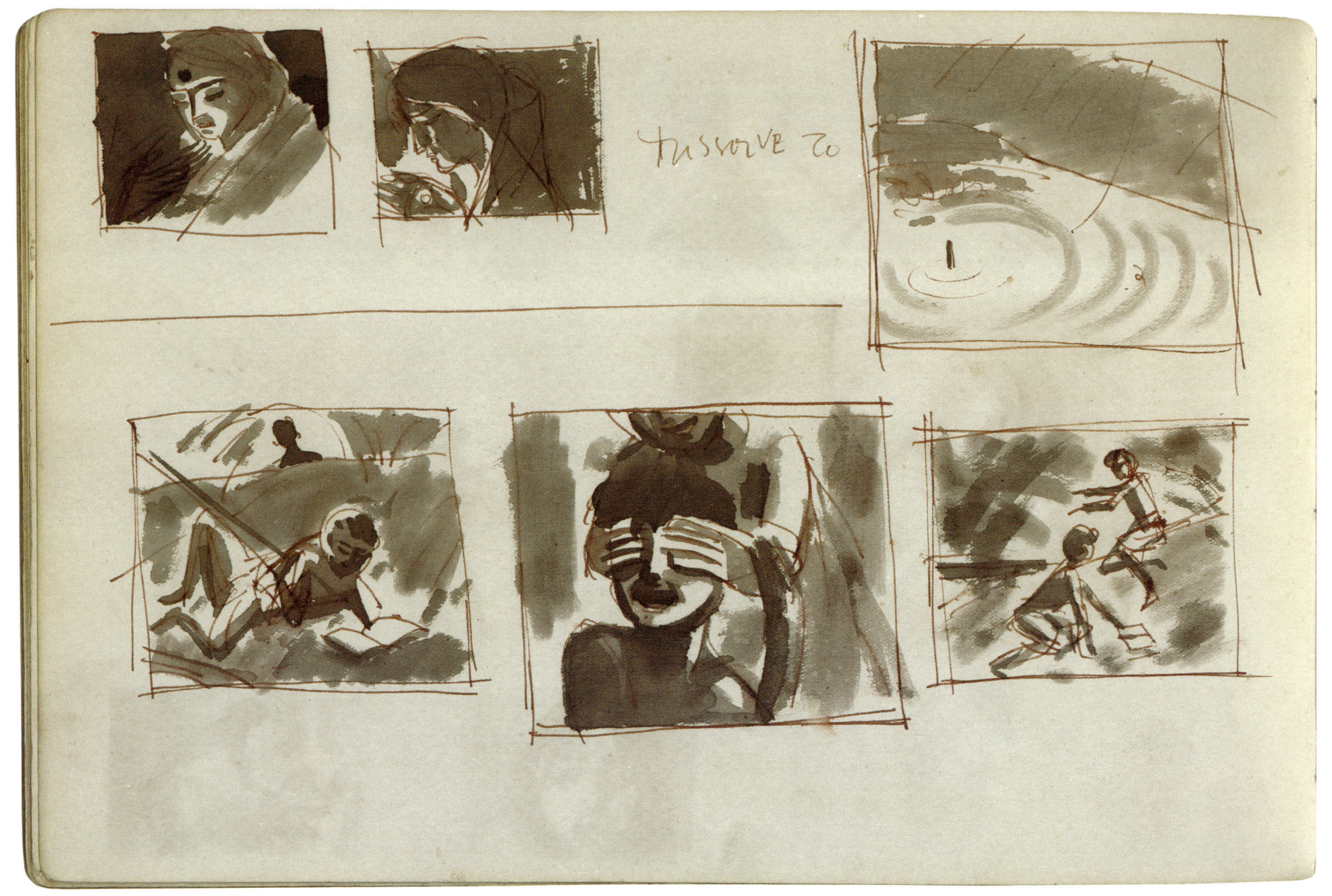

PAGE 49

PAGE 50

PAGE 51

PAGE 52

PAGE 53

PAGE 54

PAGE 55

PAGE 56

PAGE 57

PAGE 58

Captions to Sketchbook Pages*

PAGE 2: ***4 sketches (a) to (d)***: (a) Lotus among hyacinths (in a pond) / Sound of twittering of village birds on the soundtrack. When the camera tilts up, it shows: (b) Durga is reciting a rhyme. (c) Standing under a jaam tree, Durga looks up. (d) Durga picks up a stone and throws it up, aiming at the fruits.

PAGE 3: ***3 sketches (a) to (c)***: (a) Durga picks up fruits from the mud and washes them in the pond. (b) Durga tastes one, finds it sour and chucks the rest into the pond. (c) The fruits fall among a flock of ducks. Quack, quack, quack.

PAGE 4: ***4 sketches (a) to (d)***: (a) The well. (b) Sarbajaya is drawing water from the well. Beads of perspiration appear on her forehead. She is in an advanced stage of pregnancy. (c) Sejo Thakrun sits on the courtyard, watching Sarbajaya through the corner of her eyes as she prepares paan. (d) Sarbajaya pours out water from a bucket into a pitcher.

PAGE 5: ***5 sketches (a) to (e)***: (a) Sarbajaya, pitcher in her arms, proceeds towards the rear door. (b) Sarbajaya exits through the rear door. (c) Sarbajaya goes to the right. (d) The camera pans to the left and finds Durga. (e) Durga peeps from behind the wall.

PAGE 6: ***4 sketches, (a) to (d)***: (a) Durga plucks guavas from a tree. (b) Durga runs away, carrying guavas. (c) Harihar's house. Enter Sarbajaya, pitcher in her arms. (e) Sarbajaya puts the pitcher down and sits on the courtyard, panting.

PAGE 7: ***2 sketches, (a) and (b)***: (a) Durga is peeping through the side of the rear door. (b) Indir is threading a needle in her room.

PAGE 8: ***2 sketches, (a) and (b)***: (a) Enter Durga with fruits in her palms. (b) Happy to get the guava, the old lady caresses Durga by touching her cheeks.

PAGE 9: ***5 sketches, (a) to (e)***: (a) Swarna, a milkmaid, is milking her cow. Durga enters with a bowl in her hands. (b) Durga requests Swarna to give her milk. (c) Swarna continues to milk the cow as Durga holds her bowl under the cow's udders and lets Durga have half a bowl of milk. (d) Durga puts her hand inside the earthen cooking pit and gets her kittens out. (e) Sarbajaya (to Durga): 'Where did you get the fruits from?'

PAGE 10: ***3 sketches, (a) to (c)***: (a) Sarbajaya finds Indir eating a guava. (b) Sarbajaya, in pain, is forced to sit down. Indir (to Sarbajaya): 'What is the matter, my dear?' (c) Durga returns the guavas.

PAGE 11: ***4 sketches (a) to (d)***: (a) Night. Harihar's house. (b) Harihar's manuscripts, scrolls, inkpot, pen, hubble-bubble, etc. (c) Harihar is tense. (d) Durga is asleep. Harihar moves the blanket to cover Durga's body.

PAGE 12: ***7 sketches, (a) to (g)***: (a) Harihar looks at the delivery room. (b) Light falls on Sarbajaya's anguished face on the day of the delivery. (c) Durga hears the cry of a newborn baby and wonders if her kittens are wailing. (d) Durga gets up from her bed and goes out. (e) Durga looks inside the cooking pit. (f) Durga (says to herself): 'But the kittens are asleep!' (g) Durga (says to herself): 'Where is the wailing coming from?'

PAGE 13: ***4 sketches, (a) to (d)***: (a) Harihar (to Durga): 'Look, what a lovely brother you have got.' (b) Sarbajaya with the newborn in her arms. (c) Sejo Thakrun is slicing areca nuts. (d) Durga runs to inform Indir (of the news of the birth of her brother).

PAGE 14: ***4 sketches, (a) to (d)***: (a) (Durga finds) the old lady, Indir, cutting twigs in the bamboo groves. (b) 'Come home, come home, please,' Durga implores Indir. (c) Indir is singing lullabies. The baby is on the swing. Durga is seen playing behind with her kitten. (d) Apu's annaprashan. Harihar is officiating as the priest.

PAGE 15: ***4 sketches, (a) to (d)***: (a) The ceremony of Apu learning his alphabets. (a) The drum at the Charak festival. (b) Harihar and Nabin Palit are searching for Apu. (c) Apu gapes in wonder.

PAGE 16: ***6 sketches, (a) to (f)***: (a) (Apu) watches the trapeze performance by holy men at the Charak festival. (b) Harihar manages to find Apu and says to him, 'Come on, let's go home.' (c) Harihar (d) (Apu) peers through a bush. (e) A rabbit runs away. (f) Harihar points at the thorny alkushi creepers and warns Apu against touching them.

PAGE 17: ***5 sketches, (a) to (e)***: (a) Durga lifts herself behind the wall to look inside. (b) Durga returns home. Sarbajaya is cooking. (c) Sarbajaya. (d) Apu returns home and says to Sarbajaya, 'Mother, I saw a rabbit!'

PAGE 18: ***4 sketches, (a) to (d)***: (c) Durga says, 'Come along, Apu. Let me show you something.'

PAGE 20: ***4 sketches, (a) to (d)***: (b) 'Will you have a sweet, little fellow?' says Chinibas, the peddler.

PAGE 21: ***6 sketches, (a) to (f)***: (b) Sejo Thakrun, Tuni, Tepi and Nilu (c) Sejo Thakrun (to Sarbajaya): 'Is this how you bring up your daughter?' (d) Sarbajaya (to Sejo Thakrun): 'Why, what's wrong?' (e) Apu listens, a book of multiplication tables in his hands. (f) Nilu: 'Look, there is Durga.'

PAGE 22: ***3 sketches, (a) to (c)***: (a) Sarbajaya (to Durga): 'Let me examine the knot at the end of your sari.' (b) Apu listens to the altercation from his room. (c) Sejo Thakrun exits. Durga collects baichi fruits from the floor.

PAGE 23: ***5 sketches, (a) to (e)***: (a) Sarbajaya gives Durga a sound thrashing. (b) Apu, a book of multiplication tables in his hands, listens (to what is happening outside) from the room. (c) Handwriting illegible. (d) Apu goes out to look for her sister with a book of multiplication table under his arm.

* Translated by Deepak Mukerjee

REMINISCENCES

'The Whole Film Was in My Head' *

Satyajit Ray

I have no hesitation in saying that *Aam Aantir Bhenpu*, a children's edition of Bibhutibhushan Banerjee's novel *Pather Panchali*, was the source of the script of my film. I illustrated that edition. So I had to go through the book minutely. It was Dilip Kumar Gupta, owner of Signet Press that brought out the book and assistant manager of the advertising firm I was then working for, who opened my eyes to the cinematic possibilities of the first part of the novel before I thought of making a film of it.

Dilip Gupta, popularly known as DK, was crazy about films. He had his own ideas of how *Pather Panchali* should be made into a film, which roles were to be played by whom and even how certain scenes should be shot. Needless to say, DK encouraged me greatly when I decided to do the film. I, however, never told him how I conceptualized the novel as a film. I read the original novel after I had made my decision to film it.

I had scripted some Bengali short stories and novels like Manik Banerjee's *Bilasmon* and Saradindu Banerjee's *Jhinder Bandi* before I made *Pather Panchali*. But I never developed a complete screenplay for the film. As soon as I formed a broad idea, I carefully made some drawings in a sketchbook in the manner of comic strips. The sketchbook accompanied me during my visits to prospective producers. This is something I had to do a number of times as reading out scripts to producers had been a long-standing practice with film-makers.

It turned out to be a dreadful experience. I realized that there were few producers who were good listeners. Those who have no first-hand experience will never be able to appreciate how well a producer can pour cold water on the enthusiasm of a director. After listening to a script, he yawns, snaps his fingers and remarks, 'Then there is no song in your film!'

One reason why I did not do a complete screenplay for *Pather Panchali* was that I had the whole film with all its dialogue in my head. I would explain to the cameraman how a given scene should be divided into several shots for shooting purposes. Some such shots scribbled on cigarette packets might still be available if a search is made. I am told that my cameraman, Subrata Mitra, has preserved some such shots drawn on packs of cigarettes.

Till then I had not gained the confidence that I would ever be able to write good dialogue. Fortunately, there was no problem picking up the dialogue from Bibhutibhushan's novel. Three-fourths of the dialogue of the film were therefore borrowed straight from the original novel. The dialogue was given to the actors before the shooting began. They never had any problem saying their lines.

When a film is shot in a studio, an artificial atmosphere is created in accordance with the requirements of the script. On the other hand, the film-maker gets the benefit

Ray waiting for the right weather during the shoot of *Pather Panchali*. Subrata Mitra (right) is seen with his back to the camera.

* *The Statesman*, 27 April 2012. Translated from the Bengali by Arup K. De.

of many extra things that he finds strewn around him when a film is shot in natural outdoor locations. This often helps in generating new ideas, and the director has to be on the alert since there is always a possibility of such an opportunity opening up. But of course the film-maker should have the sense to judge how well a new idea may fit into the premeditated structure of his venture.

There were instances of more than one such idea developing during the shooting of *Pather Panchali*. While shooting Apu and Durga watching the train chug by, we saw the dark smoke of the train sliding down the kaash flowers. The face of the camera was immediately turned round to capture that moment. That was the last shot of the scene.

The idea of a beetle moving in the water of a pond to the strains of Ravi Shankar's sitar developed in a similar manner. There was no dearth of ponds in the village where we shot *Pather Panchali*. It so happened that we had to wait by one or the other of those ponds on many a cloudy day for the sun to come out. It was on one such day that I came upon the moving beetle in a pond and shot it at once after fitting the camera with a close-up lens. Later I felt I needed a moment in the film to use it.

Harihar has already landed a job. The scene begins with a smiling Sarbajaya receiving a letter containing the news that Harihar is coming home. Then comes a moment of delight with Durga getting soaked in the rain. This is followed with her falling ill, a dreadful stormy night, and her death. Since the story of the novel does not have any appreciable ups and downs, the film was consciously given a rhythm of its own through these events. This rhythm is absent in the novel.

The most notable feature of the novel – which, however, is its speciality – is that it reproduces the slow tempo of the uneventful life in a village faithfully. This slowness does not work for a film, which needs to have a palpable rhythm and a combination of the expected and the unexpected. That has been achieved through the sequence beginning with the joyous events of Durga Puja and the performance of a jatra. Next, Apu and Durga have a rift and immediately thereafter they exult at the sight of the train. Then Indir dies and is taken out in a funeral procession. The sequence ends with the mourning of Harihar, Sarbajaya, Apu and Durga.

A majority of the events the novel describes could not be used for the film. A large number of characters were also dropped. But the characters one is immediately reminded of at the mention of the novel have all found their way into the film.

We took considerable liberties with the character of Indir Thakrun. The novel runs to 350 pages. Indir dies on page 37. If the novel had been followed to the letter, she would have died within ten minutes of the film. The audience would surely have been disappointed with the presence of such a character as Indir for so little a time.

> 'The technique [of *Pather Panchali*] is up to Western standards and the music is beautiful. All this makes the film stand far above all Indian films which are generally mediocre.' —**Francois Truffaut**

So Indir dies towards the end of the first part of the film. In the novel, she dies when Apu is a year old. In the film, her death takes place when he is six years old. The scene where the brother and sister discover Indir's body is not there in the book. In a country where critics are always anxious to see a film follow, to the letter, the events of the book it is based on, and become hostile if they discern the minutest disharmony between the film and the story, it's a wonder that none have resented Indir Thakrun living longer in the film than she does in the novel.

The ending of the film posed the greatest problem. Harihar's home is broken, his hopes lie shattered and he leaves his ancestral home with his family for Kashi (Benares). It is a downbeat ending. It is indeed a tragedy, but there is nothing unexpected about it. So it was unlikely to have much of an impact on the viewers. Watching Harihar packing would have encouraged them to prepare to leave the theatre. How could we have them glued to their seats?

There are two incidents – one mentioned in the novel in a different way and the other not mentioned at all – that rescue the film's ending from being dull and ordinary. The sudden discovery of the string of beads stolen by Durga is the first one. In fact, Durga steals twice in the novel. First, she steals the string of beads and, thereafter, a gold box. The string is soon discovered. Apu finds the second stolen item the day before they leave Nischindipur. In the film, the string is not found when a search is made. Apu finds it the day before he leaves home along with his parents for Kashi.

It was an important incident for the film. Merely finding the string is not enough; it had to be made suggestive. So when the coconut shell noisily falls on the floor, a spider emerges from it and scuttles away. The spider has so long lived with the string of beads.

Then comes the scene of the stolen goods being thrown away. Initially I decided to show it the way it is described in the novel. But I changed my mind after watching a strange sight. One day I absent-mindedly threw a missile into a pond chock-full of thick layers of water hyacinth. Then I decided that Apu too should throw the string of beads into a pond instead of flinging it into a bamboo grove. So we see in the film that as soon as Apu throws the string, the hyacinth layers spread apart to make way for it to go down and then resume their previous position. It seems as though nature has hidden the sad tale of Apu and Durga forever in the depths of her own heart.

The second incident is the snake entering the abandoned house of Harihar. A snake has never before appeared in the film. That is perhaps why it makes an impression on the audience. The appearance of a snake is unexpected but not unnatural. The house that has been a mute witness to many joys and sorrows now turns into a serpent's den.

A New Approach*

Satyajit Ray

I think it can be stated as a general rule that the main incentive which keeps a director going with his job on a film is the hope that a great many people will pay to see the finished product and like it. In other words, he expects to make a hit and is goaded by the expectation.

That is as it should be.

Deliberately to set out to make a film for a small coterie may be all right where small private funds are involved: an avant-garde experiment in 16 mm, for instance.

But a director who is obliged to stick to normal production and distribution methods is also obliged to take into account the receptive capacities of the many other than a few.

I was aware of this fact when I set out to make *Pather Panchali*, but the prospect did not discourage me. I had my own ideas of what makes a popular film which did not, as it happened, run counter to my ideas of what makes a good film.

These ideas may well be wrong. The wide range of appeal of *Pather Panchali* may be due to reasons entirely different from what I hold them to be. But I would like to state them for what they are worth, and in the hope that contradictions may be forthcoming to further confuse the question of what makes a film click at the box office.

I have been credited with tackling a daring, undramatic, 'documentary' (synonymous with 'dry', I suppose) subject, and getting away with it.

Nothing could be farther from the truth.

* First published in *Filmfare*, 17 August 1956.

Ray looking through the Mitchell viewfinder during the shoot. Subrata Mitra (right) is seen with his back to the camera.

Pather Panchali was my first film, and I chose it because I was convinced that it was a safe subject – among the safest in all Bengali literature. I was also convinced that it was a dramatic subject, dramatic from the point of view of the screen and not the stage.

It is true that *Pather Panchali* had no clear-cut plot. But then, I do not believe that a film needs a clear-cut plot. What it needs, basically, is a theme, an idea, even a situation, perhaps a character, or a set of characters, which admits of most effective development in terms of visual images.

Pather Panchali had such a theme, a poignant human one, conveyed with all the truth and profundity that the great writer Bibhutibhushan Bandyopadhyay was capable of.

The human relationship the film depicts is of a dynamic nature. It makes possible dramatic development and interplay of characterization in the course of the narrative. Let me say at once that this interplay, this drama, is not pronounced, but subtle. Nevertheless, it is truly cinematic and, being human, it is also effective.

The background of rural Bengal was also dynamic in its changing aspects from day to day and season to season. Bibhutibhushan had made the background an integral part of his theme, which considerably heightened its cinematic possibilities.

There was, besides, the important quality of contrast. Contrasts of mood, of texture, of pace; contrast of seasons;

sunlight and shadow; sound and silence. Contrast between the beauty of the countryside and the sordidness of poverty; contrast between the children rejoicing in the meadows and the forest paths and the adults, frustrated and fatalistic, battling feebly and sporadically against hard circumstances.

Finally, but most important, the details. With his sensitive observation, Bibhutibhushan had ornamented his theme with a profusion of telling and truthful details, exciting in their possibilities of visual interpretation. I had a goldmine of film material in *Pather Panchali.*

Next came the question of approach, of finding the right cinematic style to suit the theme.

The style of the original was a wonderful blend of realism and lyricism, and I was never in doubt that I had to strive for a cinematic equivalent of it.

Visual authenticity was of the utmost importance. The characters were real, with no hint of idealisation, and they had therefore to perform against real backgrounds. This was no fad or dogma, but an absolute stylistic necessity so far as this film was concerned.

I also felt that it was worth trying to get 'atmosphere' into the film at any cost, because I believed it would heighten the drama. The subtle shades of difference between dawn and dusk, the dramatic qualities of the hot midday sun, the grey humid stillness that precedes the first monsoon shower – all these had somehow to be caught and conveyed.

This involved a respect for natural 'available' light to an extent which sometimes created tough problems for the cameraman. But undaunted, we shot nearly all the scenes on location, and as far as possible in the time of the day and season in which they were supposed to have taken place in the story.

For instance, the girl falls ill at the onset of the monsoon, and all scenes following this episode were shot on dull cloudy days, at the expense perhaps of what is known as 'pictorialism' in photography, but to the enormous gain of the overall mood. I am convinced of this gain.

The choice of new faces was also dictated by the anxiety to create believable characters. Established stars, with all due respect to them, tend to destroy the illusion of authenticity, unless they are sincere enough to shed all their well-known and well-loved mannerisms and identify themselves with the characters they are portraying. This happens only rarely, and I was happy to have a large non-professional cast.

All this meant hard work. Hard work for actors and technicians alike. We did not adopt short-cut methods, because we did not know of any. I have a feeling, which borders on conviction, that if we had adopted them, *Pather Panchali* would not have won the success that it has.

'When I first saw *Pather Panchali* in 1956 at Cannes, it struck me like thunder. When I met Satyajit Ray in 1956 in Brussels, he looked like Krishna, the mighty God. Since then he has been my great master; through him and through his works I learned how to live and how to love.'
— Kashiko Kawakita of Towa Company, distributor of all Ray films in Japan

Our Days with *Pather Panchali* *

Bijoya Ray

The memories of our excitement, passion and love associated with the making of *Pather Panchali* will never fade away.

Manik was then working for the advertising firm of D.J. Keymer. His office decided to send him to London in 1950. Maa (my mother-in-law) suggested I accompany him. Manik said he did not know how I could go with him as it was an official trip. But his office had other ideas. We were a newly-wed couple, and they said the London trip would be their honeymoon gift to us. That settled our dilemma. We went to London by ship. It was a beautiful experience, unlike any other.

We took time off to see a large number of films, including Vittorio De Sica's *The Bicycle Thief*, in London. It was the De Sica movie that gave Manik the idea of making a film of his own. Dilip Kumar Gupta ('DK' to friends and colleagues) of Signet Press had given him the assignment of illustrating a children's edition of Bibhutibhushan Bandyopdhyay's novel *Pather Panchali* before we left for London. DK was mildly put out to learn that Manik had not read the book. Manik

* The essay was originally published in Bengali in *Satyajit Ray-er Pather Panchali*, edited by Arun Sen, Kolkata: Pratikshan, 2005. Translated for this volume by Arup K. De.

'The film [*Pather Panchali*], featuring newcomers with professionals, was essentially a lyrical presentation of rural life in the raw. Shunning all the usual canons and claptrap of film material, Ray pictured with high sensitivity a poor village family's struggle for existence. ...Photographed with rigorous detail by Subrata Mitra on authentic village locales and wonderful studio sets to match, the film, though lacking in technical finish, had a soul-stirring quality.'
— Firoze Rangoonwalla, well-known Indian film critic

'I have a fascination for Satyajit Ray's films. My first experience of them was *Pather Panchali*. I was so taken with it that I sketched many drawings inspired by it. The world of the Bengali villages stirred me. My 1986 exhibition, *From Gitanjali to Pather Panchali*, was my tribute to Ray's film.'
— M.F. Husain

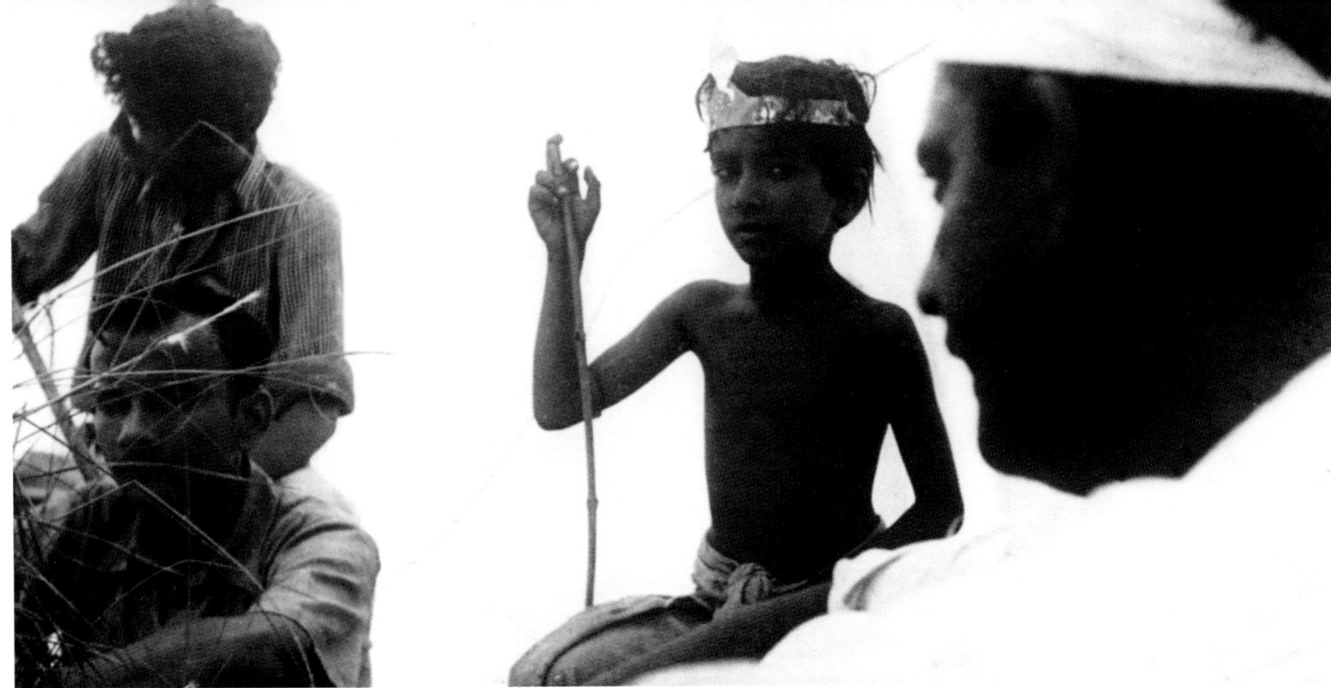

Subir Banerjee (Apu) looks at Ray (right) during the shoot. On the left are two assistant cameramen, Dinen Gupta and Nemai Ray.

did not have the time to read the book during our journey to London either. He did so while we were on our way back. Bibhutibhushan overwhelmed him, so much so that he felt it was an ideal story for cinema.

Back home, he could not wait to start preparing for the film. But it was no easy job. One needs money to make a film regardless of how little the budget may be. We raised some funds by putting all our personal resources at stake. We decided to spend whatever savings we had on the film. We disposed of our priceless music records, books on art and encashed our insurance policies. Even my ornaments had to be pawned. Anil-babu (Anil Choudhury), production controller for *Pather Panchali*, would come any time and pick up my jewellery box so that he could pawn the ornaments. We also borrowed money from close friends like Balai Chatterjee, Nirmal Chatterjee and Bula Mahalanobis. Kishore Kumar too helped us with money. A generous man, he never allowed us to pay him back.

That gave Manik an opportunity to make a beginning. But the funds petered out after some time. Then Rana & Dutt, a production-cum-distribution firm, took over the task of producing and distributing *Pather Panchali*. They also put some advertisements in the papers. But, for whatever reasons, they ultimately backed out. They also asked for their money to be returned. That stalled the shooting for the film once again.

Initially, Maa was not favourably disposed to Manik's plans to do a film. But she too relented when she saw that the work for the film had stopped midway through. She requested Bela Sen, a long-time friend of hers, to intercede with Dr B.C. Roy, then chief minister of West Bengal, on behalf of Manik. Archana, the eldest daughter of Bela Sen, had married Dr Roy's nephew. She took Manik to see Dr Roy at Writers Building, the seat of the West Bengal government. Meeting Dr Roy was almost an impossible job in those days. But the impossible became possible at Archana's intervention.

Archana did us another good turn. Dr Roy did not have much idea about films. He said funds allocation would be easier if Manik changed the ending of the film to make it a publicity statement for the panchayat department. This suggestion left Manik dumbstruck. It was, again, Archana who salvaged the situation. She told Dr Roy that the ending of a novel by so famous an author as Bibhutibhushan could not be changed in that manner. Dr Roy would not have changed his mind if Archana were not there to convince him.

The funds ultimately came from the money allocated for community development projects. The West Bengal government took over the responsibility of producing *Pather Panchali*. Thereafter, the work for the film continued without any more hitches. The film turned out to be one with a Midas touch. I have heard that the film had generated Rs 12 lakh or more in profits for its producers till 1959. When Manik heard that the film was making a profit, he requested the West Bengal government to make some payments to the technicians. But Mr P.S. Mathur, who looked after the *Pather Panchali* affairs on the state's side, declined on the grounds that there was no rule under which it could be done.

Both Maa and I were passionately involved with Manik's work. We tried to share all the anxieties and sadness and joys he experienced while working on *Pather Panchali*. We also tried to help him with his work. Subir (Banerjee), the little boy who played Apu, lived next door to us at Kolkata's Lake Avenue. I knew his mother. One day I asked my maid to call Subir in when I saw him playing with other boys on the ground floor of his house. Subir, a shy child, came in along with his elder brother. He did not say a word. We had been looking for such a boy for a long time. Subir looked admirably suitable for the role (of Apu). Manik said to him, 'You will have to work for my film.' Subir nodded his consent silently.

Later, Subir became quite at ease with us. But he was too young to do any conscious acting. In fact, he had no idea what acting was. He was made to act. Take, for example, the scene where Apu is looking for his elder sister among the kaash flowers. Manik got some people standing here and there. They called after Subir, and Subir looked in different directions. He had expressive eyes which spoke volumes. Subir and Uma (Dasgupta), who played Durga, were a study in contrast. She was intelligent and quick on the uptake. However, it was perhaps natural as she was a few years older than Subir.

It was Ashis Burman, a friend of Manik's, who discovered Uma. She was a student of Beltala Girls' High School. We contacted her father who came over to our place along with her daughter. She had on a frock and wore a pearl necklace round her neck. It was hard to imagine her as Durga, a village girl. Manik told me to help her wear a sari in the *gaachh-komor* style of a rural girl. I followed his advice, and Uma turned into Durga in an instant. Manik did not have to work much on her. She was an extraordinary actress. It's a pity she has appeared in no other film, nor has Subir.

I have already said that initially Maa did not approve of Manik making a film. Nor did she like our pawning my jewellery to raise funds. Maa wanted me to wear heavy ornaments on ceremonial occasions. So I borrowed ornaments from my sisters for such occasions. Maa did not see well at the time because she had cataract. Yet she wanted to have a look at the ornaments I wore. I'd show them to her from a distance. Later, Manik spoke of the pawning of my jewellery in an interview. Maa was shocked but by this time her disapproval had been replaced by a feeling of pride for her son. *Pather Panchali* would not have been completed but for her help.

Work on *Pather Panchali* was interrupted on more occasions than one for paucity of funds. We had to call the actors and crew members over and over again. Uma's father, who played as centre forward for the Mohun Bagan football team, grew disgusted at these interruptions. But the film gave the Government of West Bengal large amounts of money in profits over the years. Manik and his crew members got no money. But we had not bargained for what we got. Once, Manik said in jest, 'They (the government) got the money but I got fame.'

The Journey to *Pather Panchali**

Subrata Mitra

The desire to become a cinematographer dates back to my schooldays. Those days, great films used to be screened in the Sunday morning shows at Basusree or Purna theatres. My friends and I frequented the ten-anna seats to watch these films. I watched some phenomenal films at the time, the kind that impacted me a lot, particularly with respect to the photography, for example, *Les Miserables*, *Citizen Kane*, *The Magnificent Ambersons*, *The Best Years of Our Lives*, *Wuthering Heights* (all shot by Gregg Toland), *Gaslight*, *Dr Jekyll and Mr Hyde*, *Random Harvest*, *Madame Curie*, *Desire Me*, *Mrs Miniver*, *Mrs Parkington* (these by Joseph Ruttenberg), Robert Krasker's pioneering cinematography in *The Third Man*, and *Oliver Twist* and *Great Expectations* (shot by Guy Green). I watched quite a few more than once. The low lighting in films like *Great Expectations*, *Oliver Twist*, *Gaslight*, *Dr Jekyll and Mr Hyde*, in particular, impressed me a lot. I sometimes wish I could see these films again today, if only to see if they cast the same magic on me now as they did then. I am not sure if these films had anything to do with igniting in my mind the thought of becoming a cinematographer.

Mr Gopal Sanyal was a regular at these film outings with us, though of course he was older than we were. He had returned from America after working with Burnett Guffey. After every screening, we used to have long discussions with him on photography and lighting, and he used to explain a lot of things to us. He had an important role to play in my desire to become a cinematographer.

The motor vehicle licensing offices were situated behind my house. Next to these were a number of shops that dealt with facilitating photographs, filling up forms, etc., for drivers. I was six or seven years old at the time and I used to frequent the shops. The shopkeepers were fond of me and allowed me into their darkrooms and studios. The photographed faces emerging from the developing trays in the darkroom fascinated me. I am not sure what role those shops played in piquing my interest in photography.

It was in the second year I.Sc. at St Xavier's College that I began mulling over a career as a cameraperson seriously. In an era when my friends were opting for careers in medicine and engineering, the only way for me to learn camerawork was to assist a cinematographer. Dutifully, I applied for the same with a few well-known names in Kolkata. But, for whatever reason, none of them could offer me work. I find it quite ironical that I am now deeply associated with the Film and Television Institute of India, attend an American Council meeting or two every year and conduct workshops and lecture sessions for cinematography students. I love these interactions with future cinematographers, preparing them for the world. I could not have asked for anything more if I had something like the FTII when I started out.

I have heard that established cinematographers are often averse to teaching their assistants the tricks of the trade. There's this apocryphal story about a cameraman who used to set the lens exposure himself and rush to change the aperture collar as soon as the shot was done, so that the assistant would not learn about aperture issues pertaining to a shot. Of course, these days, with books on photography more easily available, things have changed. At the same time, a lot depends on the photographer's own aesthetics, though there's no denying the importance of good equipment and a knowledge of basic technique. I was unaware of so many issues pertaining to cinematography while filming *Pather Panchali* – things that a first-year student at FTII will know today. I had to literally learn my way through the making of the film, experimenting all the way, discovering things for myself. Needless to say, it called for many a sleepless night. Sometimes, I wonder if it comes too easy for students these days. With all the books, magazines, institutes at their disposal, do students today have

* Extracted from an interview published in the Bengali journal *Chitrabhash*, April-December 1980. Translated for this edition by Shantanu Ray Chaudhuri. **Subrata Mitra** was a pioneer in Indian cinematography and shot a number of Satyajit Ray's films up to *Nayak* (The Hero).

the patience for a fifteen-minute lecture on what took me thirty years to learn?

Meanwhile, after I.Sc., it was time for B.Sc., for which I had neither the desire nor the aptitude. I realized it would be a waste of time. But, given my parents' desire that I pursue a bachelor's degree, I gave in, but on one condition: the moment I got an opportunity in cinematography, I would give up college. They agreed. In fact, my parents never denied me anything I wanted to do, be it learning to play the sitar in school, or cinematography later on. If anything, a number of relatives and even the friends with whom I went on those morning shows tried to dissuade me from taking up cinematography. In fact, when work on *Pather Panchali* stalled midway, many of them said, 'Now, didn't we tell you! You should have listened to us.' Of course, I understand where they were coming from. For one, the profession was notoriously uncertain. An A-lister could somehow manage to make a living, but for run-of-the-mill cameramen, it could be tough. Also, cinema was not looked upon with respect as a profession. However, perceptions regarding a career in cinema have changed considerably, and I feel that *Pather Panchali* has a lot to do with it.

Renoir with the cast and crew of *The River*, which he shot in Calcutta

While doing my B.Sc., I came to know that acclaimed French film-maker Jean Renoir had arrived in the city to shoot his film *The River*. This was in 1950. My father took me to meet its American producer McEldowney, who said, 'I have no issues with you apprenticing on the film, but you will have to seek the director's permission.' Subsequently, I met Renoir, who too had no objections. However, he suggested that since I wanted to learn camerawork, I should work with the cameraman, Claude Renoir, his nephew. Claude Renoir expressed some doubts, given my inexperience. He said, 'You will have problems with the nitty-gritty of the work involved. No one will allow you to touch such expensive equipment.'

The film was being shot in Technicolor, involving a complicated camera. In fact, Technicolor Company had deputed two technical advisors who were responsible for handling the camera. Claude, however, had no problems with me attending the shoot as an observer. I started going to the shoot every day. The entire film was shot in a bungalow near the Ganga in Barrackpore and at Eastern Talkies Studios in Dakshineshwar. I made it a habit to record all camera movements, sketching the same, lighting patterns, etc., in a notebook.

This was my first experience of a film shoot and it was in colour! I eventually debuted as a cameraman with a black and white film. Interestingly, though Claude Renoir was a well-known cinematographer, this was the first time he was shooting in colour. There's a world of difference between today's Eastmancolor and yesteryear's Technicolor. Not only did it require a special camera which only Technicolor Company manufactured, the film speed was quite slow. It needed a lot of light. I heard that Claude had great difficulty in the absence of sufficient natural light, though I was too much of a novice to realize it on my own. Like a good student, I kept making my notes studiously, thinking it would stand me in good stead in future. Though I had little use for these notes going ahead, my notebook proved quite useful to Claude. One day, in the middle of a break in shooting, Jean Renoir happened to discover my 'priceless' notebook. Visibly happy and excited, he called for Claude. Claude too was astonished with my efforts at documenting the camerawork. A few days after this, Claude had to redo a shot. He called for my notebook and used it as a reference to get the lighting right.

Though watching the shoot was a learning experience, there was precious little I learnt about complicated aspects pertaining to lighting and camerawork. What really inspired me was the intensity and devotion that two of the world's finest film-makers and cameramen brought to their work. Making a film was almost a matter of faith with them. At that impressionable age, I could not have asked for a better initiation into cinema. It shaped my approach to cinema. My attitude to film-making would probably have been different if I had started with any other run-of-the-mill film.

It was during the making of *The River* that I first met Satyajit Ray. He was at the time art director at D.J. Keymer. Though our families knew each other, I had never met him before. He was a fan of Renoir and would make his way to Barrackpore on Saturdays and Sundays or whenever he found time to do so. Bansi Chandragupta was the art director for *The River*. Bansi-babu and Satyajit Ray knew each other. Since Manik-da did not find time to attend the shoot every day but was keen to know what was happening, I often went to his home in the evenings to discuss the film with him. He was an avid listener and expressed a great deal of interest in the photographs of the shoot that I took. He was very supportive of my photography and often told me, 'You have developed an eye.' Over time, we established a close rapport.

Around the same time I heard about his plans to make *Pather Panchali*. And he assured me that I would work on the film. However, I wasn't going to be the cameraman. Manik-da told me that he had Nemai Ghosh in mind as cinematographer and I would be his third or fourth assistant. I remember I was over the moon. In fact, I wonder if I was more happy to have been selected as assistant to Nemai Ghosh than I was when Manik-da later asked me to take over as cameraman.

However, *Pather Panchali* took some time getting started. In the meantime, Nemai Ghosh shifted to Madras and began working there. Suddenly one evening, Manik-da said to me, 'Why don't you shoot the film?' Needless to say, I nearly fell off my chair. I even tried to dissuade him. I told him that I knew next to nothing about cinematography. He responded, 'You do still photography, don't you? Where's the difference? Here, you just press a switch and the camera starts rolling. The rest is the same, isn't it?' Even if I could not reason with him that day, no sooner had the shooting commenced than we realized how different still photography was from cinematography. In the former, neither the subject nor the camera moves. In a film, everything is fluid and the lighting requirements change within a shot too. But by now it was too late to do anything.

Subrata Mitra checking the light meter as Karuna Banerjee (Sarbajaya) prepares to give a shot during the making of *Pather Panchali*

I am sure Manik-da must have been roundly admonished by his friends, relatives and well-wishers for his decision to employ me as cinematographer. As it is, this was his first film as director and he had no experience. And I was a twenty-one-year-old novice who had not even touched a movie camera. I do not blame them. I would have said the same thing if I was in their shoes. In fact, I wonder if anything remotely like this has ever happened in moviemaking circles. Yet, if I had not been asked to jump into the fire, so to speak, I do not think I could have become a cameraman. More than confidence in my abilities, Manik-da had confidence in himself. And a sense of adventure. There was probably some other reason too. Because he was inexperienced, he was a little worried about working with an experienced, well-known cameraman. When Manik-da was making the rounds of producers and distributors' offices for funds before starting the film, a number of these experienced hands had scoffed at his ideas. For example, they had laughed off his decision to shoot the rain sequence outdoors. 'You are mistaken. One does not shoot like this, it's not done,' he was told.

A lot of rumours pertaining to me went floating around in the initial days of the shoot. A number of people were convinced that I would not be able to shoot anything, or even if I did, it would not be worth the roll it was shot on! I remember vividly the experience of watching the rush print of the first day's shoot at Bengal Film Laboratory. The few moments between the lights dimming and the first shot appearing on screen seemed interminable. Even a Hitchcock film could not have been more suspenseful. While planning a shot or lighting, one often wonders if one is going about it the right way. Could it be done differently, better? Watching the kaash sway in the rush print, all such thoughts were stilled. I am not sure anyone of us would feel such joy ever again....

One of the many things that today astound me about shooting *Pather Panchali* was that we actually shot the film with a camera as heavy as the Mitchell. No cameraman today would do it. I myself won't. Yet, at the time it made no difference. We shot in the rain lugging the Mitchell, we chased grasshoppers. An Arriflex would have made it so much easier. I eventually moved on to the Arriflex with *Aparajito*, probably the first full-length feature film in India shot on the Arriflex. Manik-da and I had discussed the possibility of buying an Arriflex after *Pather Panchali*. I, of course, had no money. For *Pather Panchali*, which we shot for over a period of four years, I received a princely sum of Rs 450 per month for just three months – after the Government of West Bengal came in to finance the film. In fact, I borrowed a considerable sum of money from my father to shoot *Pather Panchali*. I remember the production manager Anil-babu telling me often on the way back home from Manik-da's, 'Subrata-babu, we need so much money tomorrow or else we won't be able to shoot.' So, it was exciting to plan buying an Arriflex with Manik-da. However, Manik-da eventually backed out, citing inability to manage funds for the same. By this time, I was obsessed with buying one, and I proceeded to do so on instalment. It is of course another matter that the twenty-month instalment was quite a pain. The camera still operates and Manik-da's latest film *Hirak Rajar Deshe* has been shot on it.

Another remarkable feature of the *Pather Panchali* shoot was that we shot almost all of it outdoors. Barring a few night shots, all sequences were shot at Boral. That called for a number of lighting innovations. We had to perforce use artificial lighting for a few indoor shots, but these were not the halogens we use today or the standard studio lights in use at the time. The Government of West Bengal had by then taken over the film. An officer at the Writers' Building assured us of being able to arrange the lighting for us. We were so cash-strapped that none of us worried about the quality of lights – that we were managing at all was a blessing. Imagine my horror when the lights arrived and I discovered that they were police searchlights! Needless to say, they were unsuitable for any film shooting. There was no way the light they cast would appear natural. So, there was no option but to use white cloth over the lights. Consider the scene where a sick Durga, lying in the room, is watching the sweetmeat seller through the window. It was necessary in this scene to have some light on Durga to balance the light on the trees, sky, outside. Moreover, the scene of Durga's death the day after was also shot with these searchlights. In contrast with the strong natural light outdoors, the light from the searchlights inside was quite weak. Yet, there was no way to balance the low light indoors with the bright one outside. We had no option but to wait for the light outside to dim.

Ray composes a scene as he looks through the camera viewfinder while Subrata Mitra prepares the scene

In the death scene you will notice that the room is lit by a lamp; outside, there's a squall. We tried our best to approximate the lights to these conditions. For the lightning, however, we desisted from using the standard process in use at the time, which involved switching a light on and off. If you observe lightning closely, the effect is more continuous; not quite a switch going on and off. To get the effect, we kept the studio lightning lights on and placed two men with cutters in front of each light. The men were tasked with shielding the lights and then removing the cutters, and that gave us the required effect.

Pather Panchali also put my music skills to test. I have already mentioned learning the sitar in school. How was I to know that it would bear fruit in the film, where I ended up playing the sitar in two scenes? The music recording for the entire film was literally done overnight. Pandit Ravi Shankar, returning to India, had written down the notations for some of the film's theme music on his plane ticket. The second tune that he played during the recording is what we know as the *Pather Panchali* theme. I had never heard a more beautiful theme music for any film till then. Today, one cannot imagine the film without this. We finished composing, rehearsing and recording the music in one night as Ravi Shankar was scheduled to leave the next day. Later, while editing, we discovered that we were running short of music in two places. Ravi Shankar was no longer available. And Manik-da zeroed in on me. I protested, citing my lack of practice. Manik-da said, 'Doesn't matter, just play.'

I composed the music that accompanies the sweetmeat seller and played the sitar for the piece – a simple piece, but it became very popular. Later, Ravi Shankar complimented me saying, 'Many people abroad have complimented me for *Pather Panchali*'s music, citing the sweetmeat seller theme in particular. I often disabuse them of the perception. But at times, I say nothing and ingeniously take credit for it.' I also played the sitar in the scene where Apu and Durga are sleeping and Sarbajaya opens a box and takes out old utensils which she would pawn the next day. By the way, I had played the sitar in two scenes in *The River* too.

Shooting *Pather Panchali* was a long struggle from beginning to end. Work stopped midway for a year and a half for lack of funds. I don't think there's a producer we did not approach – some didn't like the film at all; for others, it didn't work as a business proposition. The stories are now legion. The whole unit functioned like a family. Each member was assigned a unit – art, camera, production, etc. Yet, nothing stopped anyone from working with another department if the need arose. How can I forget Bansi Chandragupta, standing on a crumbling wall, reflector in hand, trying lighting patterns? The piece of cloth that Apu lies on was the one I had used as an infant. What both Manik-da and I struggled most against was our own inexperience. We had no knowledge of film-making. Every shot was a test that kept us awake all night. Of course, money was a problem, but even if we had money, making the film would have been as arduous a task, given our inexperience. Yet, at the end of the day, none of us will ever forget the ecstasy of working on the film.

Bansi Chandragupta in a playful mood with Subir Banerjee (Apu)

On Art Direction, Manik and *Pather Panchali* *

Bansi Chandragupta

It was in 1942 and during the Quit India movement that I gave up college. It was in my college, in Srinagar, that I had met Subho Thakur. He inspired in me the love for art and aesthetics. My family was opposed to the idea. For one, art, and that too in Calcutta. It was unthinkable. I was left with no other option but to leave home. This was in 1944. Calcutta had just gone through the horrors of the Bengal Famine the year before. I somehow managed to meet ends meet by illustrating book covers and sketching for novels that were serialized in magazines and newspapers. Thanks to Subho-babu and my experiences in Calcutta, I realized what fine art was all about. … Around this time, Jyotirmay Ray, who had made a name for himself as the story and dialogue writer for Bimal Roy's *Udayer Pathe*, requested Subho-babu for some oriental furniture design. Ray was at the time in the middle of preproduction for his new film, *Abhijatri*, and needed sets designed in the oriental style. Subho-babu introduced me to Jyotirmay Ray and I was taken on as assistant to well-known art director Botu Sen. For a salary of Rs 175 per month and free lunch on the days I reported for work. There was also a minor role in the film that I would have to essay. Needless to say, I agreed.

As luck would have it, Botu Sen fell ill with typhoid. Director Hemen Gupta and Jyotirmay Ray asked me to take over as art director for the film. I tried to reason with them that I had no experience about designing film sets, but to no avail. Following this, the film's cameraman, Arijit Sen, discussed his lighting requirements for the sets. He explained the close relationship between a film's set and lighting issues.

* Extracted from an interview published in the Bengali journal *Chitrabhash*, April-December 1980. Translated for this edition by Shantanu Ray Chaudhuri. **Bansi Chandragupta** was a pioneer in production design and worked on a number of Satyajit Ray's films.

I had few expectations of a career in cinema, but once I was in, what I saw astounded me. I realized that art direction largely involved following a few set rules without accounting for the intrinsic requirements of a scene. Art directors of the era loved to use two phrases: 'good finish' and 'good depth'. Good finish implied that any patch-up work done had been well camouflaged. Good depth, of course, meant that there was a three-dimensionality to the prop. As long as these were okay, there wasn't much to it. It used to surprise me because I believed that art direction for films should involve a great deal of thought, an awareness of the story being filmed, its location, and its characters. But most film-makers were oblivious to this. For them art direction meant nothing more than a few cardboard walls, a few window impressions etched on to them. They had no realization that the art design for a film should follow the film's screenplay, that it should have a physical persuasiveness vis-à-vis screenplay, that it was possible to design sets without cardboard or jute, that ten different rooms could be designed in ten different ways in keeping with the characters. The same sets were used in innumerable films – till they had outlived their utility. But I was merely an assistant at the time. There was not much I could do, even if I wanted to.

It went on like this for a while – working as a set designer more than an art director. It was around this time that I met Satyajit Ray through our common friend Pritish Niyogi. I had acted as a labour leader in *Abhijatri*, and Manik had praised the performance. Our friendship developed with our work on getting the Calcutta Film Society started. The society owed a lot to Manik's efforts, and I was with him in the endeavour right from the start. We watched a number of films, dissecting each film for its artistic merits. We met often at the American Library in Chowringhee. Manik used to frequent the library during his lunch hour to go through film magazines. Books on cinema were a rarity those days. Even the American Library had only a few titles. Film scholarship was largely absent – there was no realization that films needed to be read about, thought about, discussed. During these meetings with Manik, I realized how much he knew about cinema, how much he thought about it. Even before he made his first film, he was evolving as an extraordinary film scholar.

These were historic times. A new age was being ushered in, almost silently, thanks to Manik's initiative and the Calcutta Film Society. The society screened *Battleship Potemkin* in 16mm – an extraordinary experience. In 1950, his office, D.J. Keymer, sent Manik to London. In London, Manik watched ninety-nine films over a period of four months in between his office work. He wrote to me regularly about his impressions of these films. These letters gave me a glimpse of the turmoil he was experiencing in his mind. On the way back home by sea, he developed the first draft of the script of *Pather Panchali*. I still remember the trials and tribulations he had to go through to make the film, the snide remarks, and the opposition. We were all written off as a bunch of lunatics.

It was working as an assistant on Jean Renoir's *The River* that opened my eyes to the possibilities of art direction in a film. Renoir used bricks for the walls of his sets. He didn't even hesitate to use cement to create footpaths and roads for the film. It was on this film that I discovered the immense possibilities of plaster of Paris. Light yet malleable,

Pather Panchali shoot in progress. Seen from right are Subrata Mitra, Dinen Gupta, Nemai Ray and Subir Banerjee (Apu).

it could be used to create walls, staircases, ceilings. Going ahead, we used plaster of Paris for sets in *Jalsaghar* and *Devi*. I also learnt the importance of creating a believable atmosphere in art direction – it was not enough to make sets.

One of the biggest problems with designing sets in films is getting the old, washed-out look. It is easy to create a sparkling new set – a new house, new walls are easy to deliver. But to depict the ravages of time on a set calls for great ingenuity. There's a great deal of difference in the ravages wrought by time and nature and that wrought by man – and it is the former we have to approximate. I developed a technique all my own to depict the effects of rain and sun on a set: softly char the prop and then brush it well with a wire brush. Remember the door of Apu's house in *Pather Panchali*? Like old Indir Thakrun, the door too is ancient, crumbling. We made the door with pinewood, burnt it and then brushed it to get the required look. In fact, I burnt the lower part of the door a little more to depict its worn-down nature. Then we bleached the door with caustic soda. No one can tell it was a new door treated to resemble that of an old village home.

Ray directing Karuna Banerjee (Sarbajaya)

A Piece of Diamond in My Hand*

Dulal Dutta

It was raining cats and dogs. Drenched to the bone, I somehow reached Bansi Chandragupta's house, travelling all the way from Chetla. Bansi-da said, 'You're totally drenched. How will you go?' It was a Sunday morning, 27 July 1952. Bansi-da was taking me to Satyajit Ray. Manik-da was then employed in D.J. Keymer and Sunday was the only off day in the week.

Of course, Bansi-da did not tell me where and to whom he was taking me, nor for what purpose. Anyway, with the fan on full speed, I somehow managed to dry my clothes and went on foot with Bansi-da to Ray's house nearby at 31A, Lake Avenue. Bansi-da seated me in the outer room and went in. From there I heard a deep voice saying, 'Has he come? Why did you leave him outside? Bring him in.'

Walking in, I saw a gentleman in pajama-punjabi – slim and tall. Bansi-da had earlier told me, 'A friend of mine is working on a film, entirely outdoor. Will you work on it? I'll take you there on Sunday.' Manik-da said, 'I am working on a film, Bibhutibhushan Bandyopadhyay's *Pather Panchali*.'

To say that I was nervous would be an understatement. I had earlier worked on a film with Bansi-da – *Bhor Hoye Elo*. Satyen Bose was the director. I was the editor and Bansi-da was art director in the film. But I had read *Pather Panchali* many times. It was in our school course. The novel – rural background, Apu, Durga; could it be adapted into a film? After being silent for a while, I agreed. He clarified that there would be no dubbing in the film. I said okay. He said, 'I'll inform you through Bansi once work on the film begins.'

Manik-da and Bansi-da were doing some research work before starting the film. They had shot some part of the film in 16 mm but didn't like it. Then they shot about 400 feet of the film. It was to be shown in Bengal Film Laboratory. Bansi-da said, 'Manik will be there by five. You come too. We'll see a small piece.' Manik-da came exactly at five with Subrata Mitra. Of course I did not know him them. Subrata Mitra brought out a small print wrapped in black sheet from the lab. We all went upstairs and watched the film. I had by then been working in the field for a while, had assisted in many films, but had never witnessed such photography.

Manik-da said, 'What do you think?'

I replied, 'This is extraordinary.'

The scene was of a kaash forest, shot with a wall camera. Wall camera was commonly used for newsreels at the time. I only said one thing, 'You have used the same frame for "out" and "in". How will I join it?' He kept silent.

Days passed. The same year, on 20 or 27 October he started shooting, with a 35 mm wall camera. Once the print was developed, we would all watch it. I made some edits too. There was a particular tradition in Indian films before the advent of Manik-da. It was he who introduced a new trend. I found editing his film a little difficult. I had grown accustomed to working in a particular way. This was totally different. Without telling anyone, I took the help of R.D. Mehta. Saw three reels repeatedly over several nights at a stretch. Then I started editing.

The more I saw Manik-da, the more I admired him. I was even bold enough to address him as Manik-da. Given the assured manner in which he shot the film, it never felt like Manik-da was a new director, and this was his first film. I was introduced to other members of the unit. Kanu-babu, Karuna-di, Runki (the child Durga), Chunibala Devi. Shooting went on. I was living at Chetla. On his way to Boral, where

* The essay was originally published in Bengali in *Satyajit Ray-er Pather Panchali*, edited by Arun Sen, Kolkata: Pratikshan, 2005. Translated for this volume by Shantanu Ray Chaudhuri. **Dulal Dutta** was the editor on all Ray's films, from *Pather Panchali* to *Agantuk* (The Stranger).

the film was being shot, Manik-da used to pick me up. From the very first day he used to address me as 'apni'. I was with him right from *Pather Panchali* to *Agantuk*. Sandip started working with me right from his young days.

I used to go to his place, have tea. Manku-di would prepare shingara, malpoa, patisapta, which I devoured. I became a member of the family. But never did I succeed in getting him to address me as 'tumi'.

After some time, the shooting stopped for want of money. Manku-di's jewellery was pawned. Though Manik-da was drawing a monthly salary of Rs 1,800, which was quite substantial for the time, there were days when they did not even have money for regular household expenses. Editing work used to be done on Saturdays and Sundays. I used to take the tram back home, travelling second class. There were days when even that much fund was not available.

Work on the film stopped. At times I used to go to Manik-da to inquire whether he had managed to get a financier. I knew some distributors. I told them too. They wanted to hear the story. Manik-da did not even have the entire script written down – only pages of a visual script. There was a distributor called Prankeshto Datta. I knew him well. I told him. He showed deep interest after listening to the script from Bansi-da. Manik-da was not present. Prankeshto-babu agreed to finance the film. But then there was no more news from him. I felt a little embarrassed before Manik-da.

Then came Narayan Sadhukhan. By this time we had shot about 2,000 to 3,000 feet. I showed it to him. He said, 'There is no song! There should be a song by Durga.' Manik-da's reply: 'Are you crazy? Have you read Bibhutibhushan?' Sadhukhan went away. By this time there were large banners of *Pather Panchali* all over the city. But work on the film had stopped. Then Chief Minister Bidhan Chandra Roy was approached. A screening was arranged at Bina cinema hall one morning and whatever had been shot by then was shown to Dr Roy. He saw the scene where Apu and Durga, with the dog behind, follow the sweetmeat vendor – their shadows reflected in water – and said, 'What's this? Why is the picture upside down?' Manik-da smiled and introduced me. Dr Roy said, 'You, young man, keep the picture erect.'

Anyway, funds were sanctioned under the scheme of community development by the Government of West Bengal. One fine morning Manik-da called me and said, 'The film will be shown in New York. Must send it by 30 July. Get it ready.' John Huston happened to have seen the movie in a private show. It was his drive and faith in the film that took *Pather Panchali* abroad.

'When I saw the footage of *Pather Panchali* in Calcutta in 1954, I was deeply impressed and recognized it as the work of a great film-maker. My subsequent meeting with Ray was a high point of my visit to India. Everything he did and said supported my feelings upon viewing his film.'
— **John Huston**

But at the time, I was unnerved by the deadline. I replied, 'How is it possible, Manik-da? Only fourteen days are left. Some rush cutting is also pending, then the editing.' Manik-da said, 'If we can do it, it will be good for us and for Indian cinema too.' What could I do? Just said, 'Let me try.' Next morning I found Manik-da in the lab. I started working, mentally preparing myself to do so round the clock. The assistants worked overnight, with or without food, and did the sorting. Anil-babu used to come with meat and rotis – not enough food for us. Manik-da also often stayed awake all night with us.

We somehow managed to reach the airport in an official jeep, at the last moment, and loaded the cans in a plane bound for New York. Job done, Manik-da went back home as if in a drowsy stupor. I also walked down to mine.

Pather Panchali was first shown abroad. Then it released at Basusree. We had a trial show. This is called house trial. As luck would have it, a faulty segment was detected. The scene was of a labour room; Harihar loitering outside, hookah in hand. The very same night I did a patch print for that part, about 50 feet, and joined it.

Manik-da, Bansi-da, Subrata Mitra and I were seeing the film. Behind us were a few boys known to the owner of the hall. Initially, they sniggered and kept commenting on the film. On Manik-da's advice we kept quiet. At the end of the show the same boys came to Manik-da, wiping their eyes with handkerchiefs, and said, 'We have never seen a film like this before.' But my woes were not yet over. The operator with the countenance of a sahib, even wearing a tie, commented: 'Is this a film? I have never projected such a film before.' My legs, my entire body, started shivering. In keeping with the technology available at the time, I had done the patchwork on the bad part with cement – but I had not been able to do it properly, it was getting bent. We somehow managed to fix it, this time cutting out four frames.

At the first public show the next day, the entire hall was empty. Manik-da kept chewing at his handkerchief – his way of expressing tension. However, the film caught on through word of mouth. Gradually, audiences started to throng the theatre. After a week, Pankaj Dutta praised the film sky-high in *Anandabazar Patrika*. Then came news from New York, again in *Anandabazar Patrika*; *Pather Panchali* was receiving unabashed praise there. Pankaj Dutta broke down on receipt of the news from Sagarmay Ghosh. Manik-da received the news directly from *Anandabazar Patrika*. The rest is history; all our labour, all our anxiety over. It was as if I had received a piece of diamond. A new chapter began in the world of Indian cinema.

With *Pather Panchali*, Courtesy a Mitchell Camera*

Soumendu Roy

Satyajit Ray had just resumed work on *Pather Panchali*, with the Government of West Bengal as producer. I had started my career about six months ago – and was almost a novice when I joined the unit of *Pather Panchali*. I was not involved during the earlier work on the film, which Manik-da first started shooting with a wall camera. When work had to be stopped for want of funds, Manik-da met producer after producer. But he was a new director. Moreover, there was no song in the film. As usual, nobody came forward. In his own writing, Manik-da has said there was no formal script for the film. Anyway, with help from Dr Bidhan Chandra Roy, work began again.

Manik-da had hired the Mitchell camera from Technician Studio where I was an apprentice. On behalf of the studio I was entrusted with the job of looking after the camera. That is how I came in contact with him. I met Satyajit Ray, Bansi Chandragupta, Subrata Mitra and others. I did not know much about them. I had just heard about them from Kanu Banerjee – in fact, overheard, as he was talking to someone. He was saying, 'I am working on a film – Bibhutibhushan's *Pather Panchali*. Looks like it is going to be a film with a difference.' Once I joined the team – though I had little experience – I could not help feeling it was not going to be like any other traditional Bengali film. There was no artifice, no make-up; not much of hullabaloo over lights, etc., in the studio. Even the dialogues were commonplace, minimalist; as if everything was easy-going and natural.

Ray giving instructions as assistant cameramen Nemai Ray and Soumendu Roy look on

Another aspect marks the making of the film in my memory. Those days, there was a barrier in the industry. Actors and actresses, chief technicians and junior technicians – all were separate. There was little communication between the various units. Even the eating habits and food were different. But there was no distinction here. Whatever the director ate, the tea boy also got the same. This appeared very strange to me. The work style was also different. Subrata-babu, though a new hand then, had a distinct individuality in his style of working.

Two different types of actors worked in *Pather Panchali*. On one hand there were professionals like Kanu Banerjee, Chunibala Debi, Tulsi Chakrabarti, Reba Debi and Aparna Debi; on the other, there were fresh faces like Uma, Subir and Karuna Banerjee. Among technicians, Bansi Chandragupta had previous experience and a standing. All the others were new. Almost the entire film was shot outdoors – in Boral village. It was the first time I was watching outdoor shooting. The kaash scene was shot in Bardhaman district. Obviously, it was just before Durga Puja, or else how could there be any kaash forest! I remember the frenzied activity around that sequence. The scene involved a train passing by. But the location was some distance away and one had to walk quite a bit from the railway station. The Mitchell camera was a heavy one. It needed considerable manpower to carry over

*. The essay was originally published in Bengali in *Satyajit Ray-er Pather Panchali*, edited by Arun Sen, Kolkata: Pratikshan, 2005. Translated for this volume by Shantanu Ray Chaudhuri. **Soumendu Roy** has worked as cinematographer on a number of films by Ray.

Soumendu Roy (right) with Ray during the shoot

such distances. Those days there was no electricity. The camera had to be used with a 12-volt battery. I still remember running with the labourers with the huge battery on my head, lest we miss the train. There was no time even for food. Once the shooting was over, I remember Manik-da treating us with langcha, at Shaktigarh.

Gradually, my work also increased. I gained experience, got involved. Subrata-babu started assigning me work. Earlier, my job was simply to obey Manik-da's command. He would say, 'Place the camera here.' I would do that. That was all. Gradually, under Subrata-babu's watch I started adjusting the reflector, arranging the trolley and things like that. Later, in some studio shots – like the scene of Durga's death – I helped Subrata-babu in lighting. He was an extraordinary cameraman. It is difficult to use a Mitchell camera without proper training. He had never even seen one. Yet he was handling it with ease and expertise. Earlier I had heard that Nemai Ghosh was supposed to be the cameraman for *Pather Panchali*, with Subrata-babu as assistant. Nemai Ghosh had directed a film titled *Chhinnamul*. But he went to Madras and Subrata-babu joined as cameraman.

So many things come to mind in the context of *Pather Panchali* – like Indir Thakrun's death scene. Readying a bamboo platform, Manik-da asked Chunibala to lie down. Probably apprehensive that the actor might not like being carried on the shoulders, like a dead body, he said he would shoot the funeral journey later. Chunibala did not agree. She said, 'I am nearing my end too,' – she used to address him as Ray moshai or Ray saheb – 'let me be carried away on the bier. It will be best if you can lend your shoulder.' Just think of the seriousness and involvement as an actor that would make one say such a thing. Manik-da could inspire this degree of involvement from one and all. The elderly men and women who worked in the film were all from that very village. The bald-headed man in the rains was the washerman from the village.

Another memory: Manik-da was still in service with D.J. Keymer. It was difficult to get leave. There is a scene where Durga gets drenched in rain and falls sick. But the rain does not come at your bidding. Manik-da explained to Subrata-babu the kind of rain to be filmed. So, we travelled to Boral village. Subrata-babu was there, as was Shanti Chatterjee, an assistant of Manik-da's. Apu and Durga were there; also Subrata-babu's chief assistant. We waited for three days for the rain – right in the middle of the rainy season. Still, it wouldn't rain. When it came at last, after three days, Durga did not sneeze even after getting drenched. Shanti-da used to carry all sorts of things with him – thread and needle, scissors, blade – you name it, he had it. He took out a snuffbox from his pocket and thrust a pinch of snuff into Durga's nostrils. Durga sneezed.

Manik-da never lost his cool. Even when he did not like a shot, he would say, 'Oh, fine, good shot. Let's take another this way.' It was an experience to see him work. Working with Satyajit Ray and *Pather Panchali* changed my entire life. It opened up a huge vista of opportunity for me. What more can one ask for?

We Still Hum the Song of the Little Road...*

Uma Sen

It was 25 or 26 August 1955. The release of *Pather Panchali* marked a watershed in the world of Indian cinema. Completely different from contemporary films, its language and style bowled audiences over. Newspapers and journals, film academics and critics celebrated this change through various programmes and functions. Even fifty years on, it continues to overwhelm viewers. I keep getting the occasional invitation from some quarters, courtesy my role as Durga in the film – sometimes at functions like 'Remembering Satyajit' and sometimes in exhibitions on his films, or to deliver a talk on him or on opening a website in his name. All thanks to that one single film.

What is it about *Pather Panchali* that it continues to pique the interest of one and all – from the ordinary audience to film researchers? For an ordinary person like me, writing an essay in search of an answer to this question is not easy. But it may not be out of place to attempt an analysis based on my personal feelings.

Let me first come to the selection of the novel. The pre-release advertisement for the film harped on 'Unusual picturization of an Extraordinary Novel by Bibhutibhushan Bandyopadhyay'. It was unusual and extraordinary, no doubt. In the original novel, Apu's longing for an unknown and unseen faraway land is described in such poetic language that it touches the innermost chord of the reader's mind.

'...Not only to the ferry ghat – he knew this road went much farther; to the land of the Ramayana and the Mahabharata. ... That road, the verdant green, the wonderful hill range

* Extracted from an essay originally published in Bengali in *Satyajit Ray-er Pather Panchali*, edited by Arun Sen, Kolkata: Pratikshan, 2005. Translated for this volume by Shantanu Ray Chaudhuri. **Uma Sen (née Dasgupta)** played the adolescent Durga in *Pather Panchali*.

under the blue canopy surrounded by clouds – these were not in any country described in the Ramayana. Nor were Valmiki and Bhavabhuti their creators. But, in the fertile imagination of a boy in a village alive with the sound of birds chirping at dusk, in some ancient time, they were real, absolutely genuine and well entrenched.'

Reminiscing over Satyajit Ray's 'Apu Trilogy', I find that while doing the artwork for *Aam Aantir Bhenpu* – the abridged version of *Pather Panchali* published by Signet Press – Ray wanted to work on the scenario for the novel; later it developed into an intense desire to film it. Satyajit Ray captured the very same poetic mindset reflected in the novel through the childhood and adolescence of Apu and Durga, through the many trials and tribulations that a poor family in rural Bengal goes through.

When he couldn't find anyone interested in financing the film, Satyajit Ray did not give up. He started shooting it in 1952, with Rs 70,000 that he somehow raised. In that first expedition he took along Bijoya Ray, Bansi Chandragupta, Subrata Mitra, Anil Choudhury, Ashis Burman, Asit Sen and his Mitchell camera, besides Subir and me.

Uma Dasgupta (Durga) plays a prank on Chunibala Devi (Indir Thakrun) as Ray, Subrata Mitra and Nemai Ray (from left to right) look on

The location was chosen with great care. The novel had as its background the village Gopalnagar where the author grew up and became a teacher. Initially, Satyajit Ray took some shots there – Apu and Durga running through the kaash flowers to see the train. Due to various problems, however, those 1952 shots could not be incorporated in the final film. Work on the film had to be stopped midway for dearth of money. Work resumed with new vigour in 1954 in the village Boral, not far from Calcutta. It is now a bustling township.

None of the actors in the film, barring Kanu Banerjee, was a professional. That is probably why the film's surroundings and its characters come across as so fresh, so natural. Subir (Apu) was so young that he had to be literally cajoled into acting, with inducements and by explaining everything that he needed to do. Yet the innocence of his face, the way it conveys feelings and emotions, through frequent blinking of his eyes, created such an enthralling portrait, thanks to Satyajit Ray's magic wand.

Subir and Chunibala Devi received international awards. The film too. I was in a sort of trance those days, receiving felicitations from many places. Even now, I feel overwhelmed remembering those days. I have read in the newspaper that when those scenes of Nischindipur, Sonadanga's fields were being screened in New York's Fifth Avenue, students were given tickets on discount. The reporter also wrote: '...seventeen US magazines have listed Uma Dasgupta the thirteen-year-old handsome Durga of the film as one of the teenagers of the year.' I must confess without any doubt that the major credit for the thirteen-year-old Durga becoming one of the topmost teenagers of the year must go to Satyajit Ray.

Thinking of those days makes me nostalgic. Take the scene of Indir Thakrun's death. Durga and Indir Thakrun share a mutual bond that goes beyond the usual aunt-niece relationship. Both are victims of Sarbajaya's sharp tongue and unwitting cruelty. Durga first experiences death through that of the most beloved person in her life. Just think of that scene: Apu and Durga playfully running along the jungle track, reciting nursery rhymes. Seeing her aunt sitting alone in the bamboo grove, Durga goes forward. With what precision Manik-da explained how pathetic this death was to Durga! How in a whispering tone Durga calls 'Pishi, Pishi, Pishi', gets no response, shakes her a little, and the aunt's body tumbles. Manik-da instructed me on how to convey an expression of bewilderment at the shock mingled with helplessness. He was happy with my performance. But I just could not do the next scene – Durga silently weeping at Indir Thakrun's verandah. But genius that he was, Manik-da managed to overcome this shortcoming on the part of the actor by capturing Durga's tearful eyes in chiaroscuro, creating a mournful ambience…

Subir Banerjee (Apu) and Uma Dasgupta (Durga) relax in between their shots

Manik-da worked on my performance sequence by sequence, one at a time. Take, for example, the scene of the theft of Tuni's garland of beads. A humiliated Sarbajaya is beating Durga mercilessly. Manik-da advised Karuna-di not to think of my getting injured but to go on beating me, pulling me by the hair and throwing me out. Everyone remembers Karuna-di's extraordinary performance in that scene as, driven by anger and humiliation, she loses all sense of proportion. Just think of the scene: I am wilting under the assault. The cacophony causes Apu to blink. (Shanti-babu made a loud noise with the reflector to make Apu blink. Subir was such a little boy! How could he convey that otherwise?)

The scene of Durga getting drenched in rain. The strains of Raga Desh on the sitar in the background. Durga swinging her hair around in the rain and making faces at Apu. Manik-da had taken a few stills of mine with my tongue protruding when I first met him. We had to wait for a long time for the rain. We used to spend long hours chatting under a tent of plastic sheets. In Bibhutibhushan's words: 'The sky is overcast with rain-bearing cloud…' Then, '…all around it is only the pitter-patter of falling rain – noise … branches shaking in the breeze … Apu grinding his teeth with cold…' Durga pulled him closer and, as a last resort, started chanting … *Nebur patay karamcha, he brishti dhore ja…*' While filming this I was supposed to sneeze several times. But during the first few shots I could not get it right. Finally, Shanti-babu helped me with a pinch of snuff.

Durga and Apu following the confectioner (Srinivas), a dog following them, walking by the side of a pond. Their reflection in the water below, a folk tune in the background. They are going towards Ranu's house. The dog was not following us properly. So Manik-da gave some eatables in my hand to carry, off camera. The dog now kept to the script.

Test photos of Uma Dasgupta taken by Ray on the rooftop of his Lake Avenue house

… Manik-da had the different sequences clearly etched in his mind. He used to draw the sequences shot by shot, illustrate them and write alongside in his notebook. He used to give us the script but told us, 'Don't commit to memory, I may change it.' …

And who can forget the music by Ravi Shankar? The separate themes he composed were so beautifully fused with the scenes by Satyajit Ray himself. The use of Raga Desh in the scene of Durga and Apu getting wet in the rain, Raga Tori in Durga's death scene, Raga Patadip on the dilruba when Sarbajaya breaks down while informing Harihar of Durga's death reveals the director's knowledge of music and the skill with which he assimilated it in the film.…

Pather Panchali was in the making for a long time, thanks to fund crunch and many other problems. During that entire period the whole unit worked like a single family. For me, the days of shooting were a relief from monotony. Everyone used to look after us, give us sufficient importance. Satyajit Ray gradually became Manik-da for all. As an adolescent, I did not even realize the importance of the work all of us – Khoka-babu (Dinen Gupta), Roy-babu (Soumendu Roy), Shanti-babu, Bansi-babu, Subrata-babu, Karuna-di, Subir, Anil-babu, Rama or Neela Mishra in Ranu's role, many others and me – were involved in.

Learning from experience, Manik-da probably realized the problems of working with new faces. So, it is said, in his later films he preferred less of new artists. But then Soumitra, Sharmila and Aparna also made their first films with Manik-da. By virtue of their talent, they went on to rule the minds and hearts of their fans. Manik-da was perhaps their philosopher's stone. And we – from *Pather Panchali* – still hum the song of the little road.

The film received twelve international awards in all during the ten-year period from 1956 to 1966. In 1955, it was awarded the President's Gold and Silver Medals. As the film was produced by the Government of West Bengal and under Dr Bidhan Chandra Roy's patronage, we were also felicitated and awarded silver medals. Young writers and journalists arranged a huge felicitation programme at the Senate Hall. Several organizations congratulated us.

But there were detractors too. I heard Bhanu Bandyopadhyay never said anything good about the film. Nargis Dutt also made some uncharitable remarks about it. Something like better not to showcase such poverty to the world. But that was the reason why *Pather Panchali* was felicitated as 'the greatest human document'. Because the English version of the title was 'Song of the Road', Dr Bidhan Chandra Roy perhaps thought the film could be used in depicting community development projects of the government; and that is why the financial help was forthcoming. There are many such stories about *Pather Panchali*. Even the other day, in a leading newspaper, below my photograph my name was written not as Uma Dasgupta, not as Runki Banerjee (the one who played the infant Durga), but as Rinku Banerjee. Who knows wherefrom they get such news! Many journalists ask such silly questions, that too on telephone, it appears they have neither read the book nor seen the film.

I have no regrets. The poet and writer Sunil Gangopadhyay has written in his poem that while watching the film he transforms himself into Apu; his childhood resembled Apu's. Artist Bikash Bhattacharya held an exhibition titled 'Durga'. In the publicity booklet, he wrote that he visualized Durga in every girl. Sometimes she is a daughter, sometimes a wife, sometimes a mother – sometimes it is only 'She'. He knows that the Durgas of the world never lose. Subrata Mitra took me to that exhibition.

This is how people at every level of society relate to the experience of watching *Pather Panchali*. They do not allow me to forget the experience. Manik-da felt there were some shortcomings in the picturization of *Pather Panchali*; that he would correct these given a chance. Despite these shortcomings, even today, after years, *Pather Panchali* is a matter of pride for all Bengalis.

Still Apu after All These Years*

Subir Banerjee

It was perhaps 1951 or '52. We were living in Lake Avenue. Satyajit Ray was our next-door neighbour – already a well-known name, a commercial artist in D.J. Keymer, son of Sukumar Ray. Of course, I was too small at the time to know all these. I only knew that the kakababu next door was a tall man – to look at him one had to bend

Subir Banerjee (left) with his elder brother. Photograph by Ray.

one's head sufficiently backward. One morning I was playing in the compound. Suddenly, someone from the house next door – perhaps their domestic help – smiled at me and said, 'My boy, Dadababu is calling you.' Who was this Dadababu? I had no idea. Could it be a child lifter? Taken aback, I just ran to my mother. Mother came out and inquired why he was asking for me. The man said, 'Dadababu wanted me to bring him. I don't know why.' My parents knew Satyajit Ray. They decided to let me go – not alone but with my elder brother.

* Extracted from an essay originally published in Bengali in *Satyajit Ray-er Pather Panchali*, edited by Arun Sen, Kolkata: Pratikshan, 2005. Translated for this volume by Shantanu Ray Chaudhuri. **Subir Banerjee** played Apu in *Pather Panchali*.

I saw two beautiful ladies sitting there. Later I learnt that the elderly lady was Suprabha Ray, Satyajit Ray's mother. The other one was Bijoya Ray, his wife – I would come to call her kakima. Thakuma (Suprabha) kissed me and offered toffee to both of us. I was feeling a little nervous but now all fears vanished. A little later the huge, tall kakababu came in – the one I frequently saw from our verandah. Thakuma smiled and said, 'Manik, you have been looking for Apu all over Calcutta. And here he is, next door, you never noticed! Look, I have brought your Apu.' Kakababu looked at me for quite a while, turning me this way and that, the way a photographer observes his subjects. Then he asked me my name, which school and class I was in, and all that. He said, 'Come to the roof with me. I'll take photographs of you both.' He photographed both of us on the terrace of his house. (I have preserved that photograph taken by Satyajit Ray with me to this day.) We returned home thereafter. Later I learnt that Kakima used to observe me playing in the verandah of our house. In a way it was she who first thought of the possibility of casting me as Apu. She herself was a good actor and singer. Hers was no mean contribution behind the creation of *Pather Panchali*.

They picked me for Apu, but the real problem came now: convincing my parents. My father, Shantimay Bandyopadhyay, and mother, Jharna Bandyopadhyay, knew Satyajit Ray as a great artist. He was making a film, fine. But they could not think of letting their son act in the film. Acting in films was not as commonplace then as it is now. People in that era prioritized their children's education and career – instead, here was a proposal for acting in a film! How could that be allowed? Even though Father relented, it was difficult with Mother.

As a last resort, Mother took me to Giridih, to my maternal uncle's place, during the Puja holidays – in a sense, fled with me from Calcutta. She would never allow her son to act in a film. But to no avail. Satyajit Ray took our address from Father and sent his production controller, Anil Choudhury, to Giridih to bring me back. And bring me back he did.

Subir Banerjee (Apu) playing with the camera as Uma Dasgupta (far left) prepares for her take

We returned to Calcutta. Then, one day, Kakababu came to our place and had a long conversation with my parents. I don't know how he convinced them. But certain things that I learnt after growing up are still etched in my mind. Kakababu had said, 'Why are you hesitant to allow your son to act in a film? It's taken me so long to find my Apu. I have seen over two hundred boys, but couldn't find anyone suitable. The film won't be possible without him.' Then he said something that my parents could not disregard. He said, 'I'll make a film that will alter the course of Bengali film-making. Today no one knows your son or me. But a day will come when the whole world will know us.' Imagine the self-confidence and far-sightedness a director must have to say something like this even before starting work on his first film.

So much has been written about *Pather Panchali*; so many debates, so many screenings. Even today the film enthralls the audience, stirs them as it did sixty years ago. ... The intimate relation between man and nature that Bibhutibhushan wrote, Kakababu presented beautifully. I was not old enough at the time to appreciate all these. Nor was I supposed to. I have since then watched the film so many times – and each time I am overwhelmed with newer joys, I discover newer meanings.

Take the scene where Harihar returns home with a sari for Durga. The house has been devastated, Durga is dead. In this scene, Kakababu does not show only Harihar and Sarbajaya. The camera pans over the entire house, destroyed by nature's fury. The fallen house and Durga's death merge. As if the natural storm is a harbinger of the storm that befalls this small, poor family. … It is as if the struggle of all the deprived people of the world, their hopes and desires, are manifested in this scene. That is why *Pather Panchali* is ageless. That is why it is prized as a 'great human document'. That is why even after sixty years we can undoubtedly say, *Pather Panchali* was, still is, and will remain. The appeal of *Pather Panchali* is eternal.

Let me say a few words about the shooting. I felt as if we were going on a picnic. There was no fear or anxiety. It was all pure joy. There used to be gaslight in Calcutta streets those days. And large taxis – Studebakers, etc. There was a Sikh driver – I still remember his name – Bachchan Singh. Every morning we used to take the car to Boral and return by evening. Not that we had to work the whole day. Monkeys were a nuisance. Once, they threw green coconuts on our car, denting its hood. I remember, I was never served outside food, lest I fall sick. Kakima used to carry specially prepared food for me. It was a homely atmosphere. I was so small that I do not remember everything well. I didn't even realize what a classic film I was being part of. The shooting went on for three years, interrupted now and then for want of funds.

I was nine when the film released on 26 August 1955. Later, I received many more offers for acting in films. But my parents did not agree. I feel proud of having been associated with the timeless work – *Pather Panchali* – which remains my only film. Even after the lapse of half a century, I get an occasional invite to some function or am asked to write a piece for a newspaper or journal, only because of this one film. I feel proud of myself. I have received such fame and love that I never felt like acting in another film ever. I just want to live with the identity of that eternal 'Apu'.

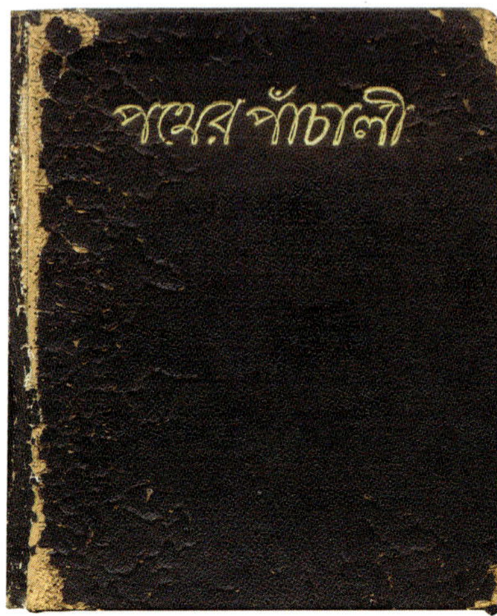

Ray's personal copy of *Pather Panchali*, the iconic novel by Bibhutibhushan Bandyopadhyay. This copy, signed by the author, is a 6th edition print (1945) and was published by P. Mitra and Company. The novel was first published on 2 October 1929 by Sajanikanta Das under the imprint of Ranjan Prakashalay.

Ray's sketch of Bibhutibhushan Bandyopadhyay for the Park-ink advertisement

POSTSCRIPT

C
O
P
Y

KODAK LIMITED
P. O. Box No 9086
17, Park Street
Calcutta 16

SOLD TO:
J. Walter Thompson Co. (E) Ltd.
5, Bankshall Street
Calcutta

Invoice No CC/5803 dated 23-4-55 Your Order of - Office Order No 9831

A/C 'PATHER PANCHALI'

Item ① 12,000 Feet. 'Kodak' 35mm Fine Grain Duplicating Positive Safety Cine Film Emul. No: 5365-221 per foot Rs 0.10 1200- 0- 0

Bengal Sales Tax on Rs 1140/- 53- 7- 0

1253- 7- 0

Goods sent to:

Sri Satyajit Ray
31/A, Lake Avenue
Calcutta

The Proprietors of

BINA AND BASUSREE

request the pleasure of the company of
Shri Satyajit Roy & Shrimati Roy.

AT A RECEPTION TO MEET

Shri Satyajit Roy, Director, Artists and Technicians
of **"PATHER PANCHALI"**
at BINA 219, Cornwallis Street,
on Sunday the 25th September, 1955, at 9-30 A. m.

Dr. H. C. MOOKERJEE, Governor of West Bengal and Dr. B. C. ROY, Chief Minister of West Bengal will grace the occasion by their presence

Special Show of "PATHER PANCHALI"

Please present this Card at the Gate.

Above: Letter of invitation for a special show of *Pather Panchali* organized by the proprietors of Bina and Basusree cinemas
Left: The invoice for the raw stock bought for the shoot of *Pather Panchali*

POSTERS

Ray used to design the posters of his films himself. For posters, two standard measurements were in vogue during the time and he used to design them in actual dimensions.

Far Left: The Bengali poster for *Pather Panchali*, measuring 30'' x 40 ''
Left: The English poster for *Pather Panchali*, measuring 30'' x 40 ''

BOOKLETS

বিভূতিভূষণ বন্দ্যোপাধ্যায়ের

॥ পথের পাঁচালী ॥

পশ্চিমবঙ্গ সরকারের নিবেদন

পরিবেশন। অরোরা ফিল্ম করপোরেশান লিঃ

। চিত্রনাট্য ও পরিচালনা ।	। সঙ্গীত ।	। আলোকচিত্র গ্রহণ ।	। শিল্পনির্দেশক ।
সত্যজিৎ রায়	রবিশঙ্কর	সুব্রত মিত্র	বংশী চন্দ্রগুপ্ত
। সম্পাদক ।	। শব্দগ্রহণ ।	। ব্যবস্থাপনা ।	। সঙ্গীতগ্রহণ ।
দুলাল দত্ত	ভূপেন ঘোষ	অনিল চৌধুরী	সত্যেন চট্টোপাধ্যায়

॥ সহকারীবৃন্দ ॥

পরিচালনায়। শান্তিকুমার চট্টোপাধ্যায়, আশীষ বর্মন, সুবীর হাজরা।

আলোকচিত্র গ্রহণে। দীনেন গুপ্ত, নিমাই রায়, বীরেন ভট্টাচার্য, সৌমেন্দু রায়।

শিল্পনির্দেশনায়। সুরেশ চন্দ্র, সুরৎ বর, দিবাকর দত্ত।

সম্পাদনায়। সুকুমার সেনগুপ্ত, তপেশ্বর প্রসাদ, হরিনারায়ণ মুখোপাধ্যায়।

ব্যবস্থাপনায়। সুরেন সাহু, সত্য, নটবর, বাদল, দুলাল।

॥ পরিস্ফুটন ॥

বেঙ্গল ফিল্ম ল্যাবরেটারিজ লিঃ

॥ ভূমিকালিপি ॥

হরিহর।	কানু বন্দ্যোপাধ্যায়	ডাক্তার।	হরিমোহন নাগ
সর্বজয়া।	করুণা বন্দ্যোপাধ্যায়	চক্কোত্তি।	হরিধন নাগ
দুর্গা (বড়)।	উমা দাশগুপ্ত (অ্যাঃ)	দাসীঠাকরুণ।	নিভাননী দেবী
অপু।	সুবীর বন্দ্যোপাধ্যায়	পুরোহিত।	ক্ষীরোদ রায়
দুর্গা (ছোট)।	রুণ্‌কি বন্দ্যোপাধ্যায়	রাণু।	রমা গঙ্গোপাধ্যায়
সেজোঠাকরুন।	রেবা দেবী	টেঁপি।	মঞ্জু
নীলমনির স্ত্রী।	অপর্ণা দেবী	সতু।	শ্যামল
প্রসন্ন গুরুমহাশয়।	তুলসী চক্রবর্তী	টুনি।	পুতুলরাণী
বৈদ্যনাথ মজুমদার।	বিনয় মুখোপাধ্যায়	পুঁটি।	পাপিয়া
চিনিবাস ময়রা।	হরেন বন্দ্যোপাধ্যায়	বিনি।	অপর্ণা (ছোট)

ভারত ফোটোটাইপ স্টুডিও, কলিকাতা-১২ হইতে মুদ্রিত

Pather Panchali

The Story of Apu & Durga

The film tells the story of a poor Brahmin family who live in their ancestral village in Bengal : the father (a poet and lay priest, an optimist and dreamer whose unrealistic approach to life keeps his family in humiliating poverty) ; the mother (a practical woman who must cope with the everyday struggles of the family) ; Durga (their daughter, about six years old when the film begins, whose one bad habit is stealing mangoes from the neighbors' orchards) ; Apu (their son, an intelligent boy much indulged by mother and sister) ; an aged aunt (who lives in a hut in the garden, constantly bickering with the mother but beloved by Durga).

Secondary characters are : a rich, cantankerous woman (who owns most of the surrounding orchards and who makes no secret of her disdain for the poor family) ; a sympathetic woman (a friend of the mother).

Early in the film Apu is born. Later, the father, sitting in the kitchen, tells his wife of his new job in the Treasury and Plants a wonderful future : he will repair the house, find a husband for Durga, send Apu to a good school, and write a great poem or play. The mother is infected by her husband's optimism.

Six years pass. The father is still drudging at his underpaid job ; the house is unrepaired. Apu attends a poor school run by a scholar who is also the willage grocer. The mother, tired for her husband's complacency, urges him to assert himself.

The children visit the house of the rich, cantankerous woman who later accuses Durga of stealing a valuable necklace. Durga is searched but the necklace is not found. The rich woman accuses the poor family of thievery. The mother vents her humiliation and rage by throwing Durga out of the house......but later sends Apu to bring her home.

That night while the old aunt tells a fairy story to the children the father returns with his overdue wages and tells of an offer to officiate at an initiatior ceremony for which he will be well paid. The mother urges him to set out immediately, bet he insists that delay is more seemly.

After a bitter quarrel with the mother, the old aunt leaves the house. Meanwhile the children attend a travelling fair and theatrical performance, quarrel and are reconciled. The old aunt returns home ill and begs to be allowed to die there, but the mother does not believe her and refuses to take her in. The old woman leaves. The children find her in the orchard, but their joy is turned to sorrow when they realize she is dead.

The father finally sets out for the initiation ceremony. The mother's anticipations of prosperity are shattered by the arrival of a postcard : the ceremony has been cancelled ; her husband is going to the city and will not return until he has earned enough money to repair the house.

Months pass. The lovely daughter of the rich, cantankerous woman is married. Durga is impressed and begins to perform religious rites (planting the flower). The mother fights a losing battle against poverty.

A second postcard from her husband brings good news—he has earned the necessary money and is returning home.

The homecoming is saddened by Durga's death. The father at last faces life realistically and decides to take his family to Benares.

The family leave their ancestral home for a new life.

॥ কাহিনী ॥

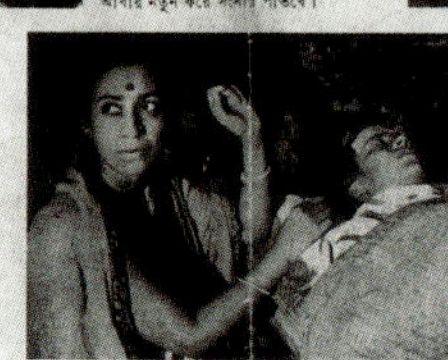

Above: The folded booklet of *Pather Panchali* designed by Ray himself

Far Left: The booklet consisted of the iconic cover, the cast and crew in Bengali (upper half) and summary of the story in English (lower half)

Left: The inside fold of the booklet had the summary of the story in Bengali along with stills from the film

"LA COMPLAINTE DU SENTIER"
Adapté du roman de
BIBHUTIBHUSHAN BANDOPADHAYA.

Réalisateur	SATYAJIT RAY
Production	West Bengal Government
Musique	RAVI SHANKAR
Cameraman	SUBRATA MITRA
Art Director	BANSHI GUPTA
Montage	DULAL DUTTA
Ingénieur du son	BHUPEN GHOSE

Interpretation

Le père	KANU BANDO-PADHAYA
La mère	KARUNA BANDO-PADHAYA
Apu	SUBIR BANDO-PADHAYA
Durga	UMA DAS GUPTA
La tante	CHUNIBALA

"LA COMPLAINTE DU SENTIER" est une adaptation du célèbre roman de BIBHUTI-BHUSHAN BANDOPADHAYA — "PATHER PANCHALI".

Déjà en 1945, SATYAJIT RAY avait illustré ce livre. Enthusiasmé, il décida avec quelques amis de le filmer en investissant leurs propres capitaux.

Cette entreprise fut menée dans un esprit d'aventure par un groupe d'amis sans aucune formation professionnelle. (RAY était directeur artistique pour le compte d'une maison de publicité et son cameraman, SUBRATA MITRA, était un photographe amateur.)

Le premier de manivelle fut donné en octobre 1952. Les méthodes de travail étaient imposées par le manque d'argent: tournage en extérieur avec des acteurs non professionnels.

Au bout de trois mois, les capitaux firent défaut. Pendant près d'un an RAY et ses amis furent voués à l'inaction. Néanmoins, le gouvernement du West Bengal, après vision des premiers rushes, prêta son aide financière au réalisateur.

De cette manière, le film a pu être terminé en mars 1955 et fut projeté pour la première fois en août 1955.

● For distribution in United Kingdom, Commonwealth, Europe, South America, Japan, Middle East, Far East, Soviet Union, China and Eastern Democracies
Write to : HITEN CHAUDHURY PRODUCTIONS, Film Centre, Tardeo Road, Bombay, India.

New Jack Printing Works Private Ltd., Bombay 13.

LA COMPLAINTE DU SENTIER

PATHER PANCHALI

DANS UN VILLAGE DU BENGALE L'ADOLESCENCE ET L'ENFANCE MELENT LEURS EMPREINTES AVANT DE SE SEPARER ET REDECOUVRENT POUR NOUS LES GESTES QUOTIDIENS QU'ON AVAIT OUBLIES.

Resume Du Scenario

Dans un village bengali, une famille indienne vit chaque jour la simple et difficile aventure de la vie.

Tandis que DURGA, la petite fille, découvre les grands arbres de la forêt, l'aieule, courbée par l'âge, târtonne son existence de vieille femme et croque ses dernières mangues.

La mère, tendue par le travail, porte sa réponse sévère aux exigences de ceux qui l'entourent.

Le père, éloigné de la vie domestique, revient à la maison s'approvisionner en reconfort.

Un petit garçon naît. Les années passent.

La berceuse que chantait l'aieule deviendra son tranquille chant de mort.

APU, le petit garçon, a maintenant huit ans et DURGA est une jeune fille.

Tous deux découvrent grâce à DURGA le sens de la vie, et leur complicité naît de la mutuelle attention qu'ils portent aux gens, aux bêtes et aux plantes.

Le père s'en est allé à la ville et l'argent vient à manquer.

Les pluies de la mousson privent APU de sa soeur.

Resté seul au milieu de son univers ruiné, il part avec ses parents qui tenteront de trouver à Bénarès la paix vers laquelle ils ont tendu leur existence.

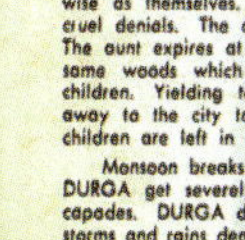

Story

Adolescence and childhood mingle their footprints before separating, and rediscovers for us the forgotten expression of everyday life in a remote Bengali village.

The family is small: DURGA, the little girl; her mother, ever harassed by drudgery and indigence; her father, indifferent to domestic duties, easy going in 'respectable' service which yields less than subsistence wages and her aged aunt, pining for release in death from mortal misery. It was a typical middle-class family of rural Bengal.

Years pass. A son is born. DURGA is happy.

APU, the son, is now six years old; DURGA, almost grown up.

The children roam around, uncared and uncaressed, in woods overgrowing on fallow lands abandoned likewise as themselves. Nature compensates them for life's cruel denials. The children come to face realities of life. The aunt expires at last, in melancholy frustration, in the same woods which afforded enlivening bounty to the children. Yielding to his nagging wife, the father goes away to the city to make money. The mother and the children are left in dismal gloom and crushing poverty.

Monsoon breaks in torrential downpour and APU and DURGA get severely drenched in one of their mad escapades. DURGA dies of it. APU is left alone. Raging storms and rains demolish the tottering structure which had been their ancestral home since generations past.

The father returns in high spirits, ignorant of the blows to his family by death and destruction. He decides to leave the village for good.

And so, alone in his shattered world, APU goes with his parents to the far-away city of Benares in quest of the peace they did not find in their old village.

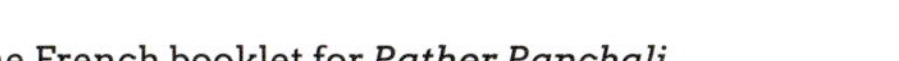

The French booklet for *Pather Panchali*

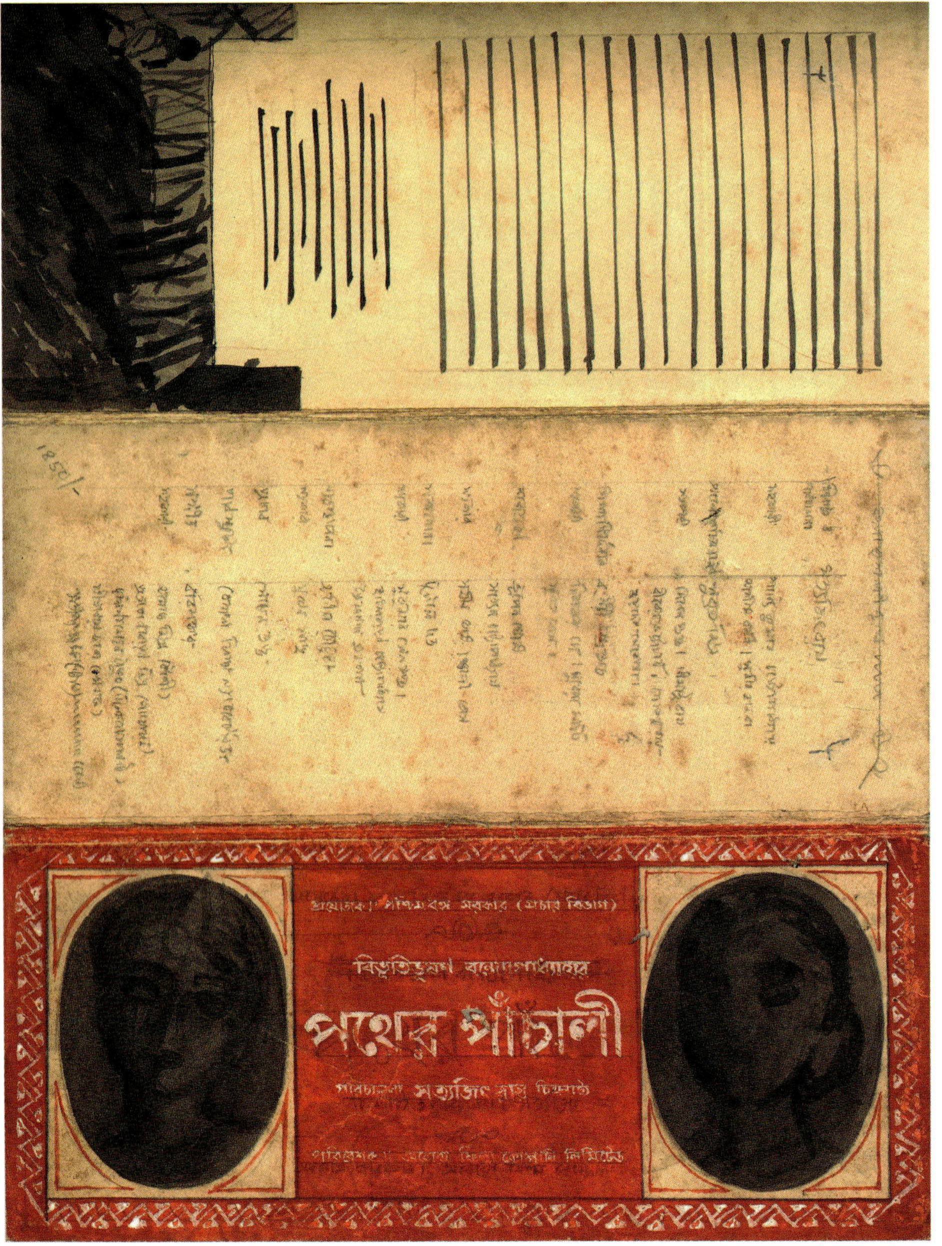

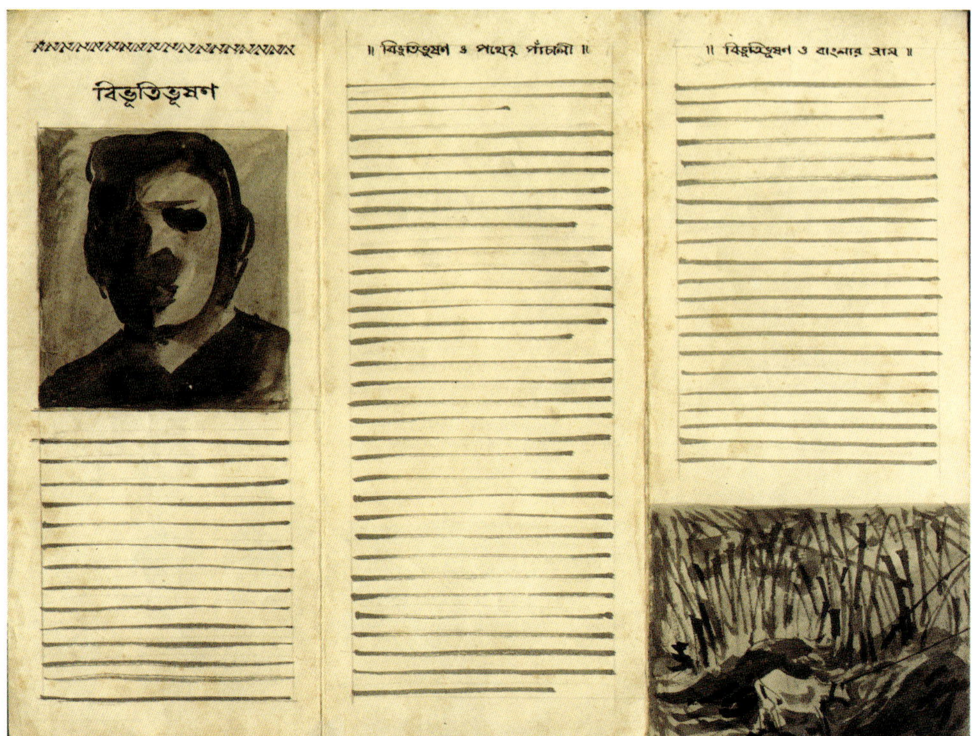

Above: The outer flaps of the trifold booklet for *Pather Panchali* that Ray planned and designed meticulously, but it was never printed, primarily due to lack of funds

Right: The sequence of the hand-drawn booklet (inside flaps) included a detailed plan for placement of text along with movie stills

The unprinted booklet included a stunning gallery of characters from *Pather Panchali*, drawn by Ray himself

DRAFT SCENARIO

Satyajit Ray said that he had never made a full-fledged script for *Pather Panchali*. In fact, he did more than one draft script for his maiden film. One of them had been written before he made the now-famous visual screenplay. But later he felt that his Bengali was inadequate, and so requested his friend Ashis Burman to rewrite the dialogue in the script. Then he went through Bibhutibhushan Bandyopadhyay's novel once again. This time he felt that the dialogue the author had written for his novel was ideal for a script. So he wrote another draft script. But he used neither of these two scripts while making the film. The first draft was published in a Bengali magazine entitled *Sakal* in 1992. The pages of the script published here have been culled from the second draft that Ray made.

Debasis Mukhopadhyay

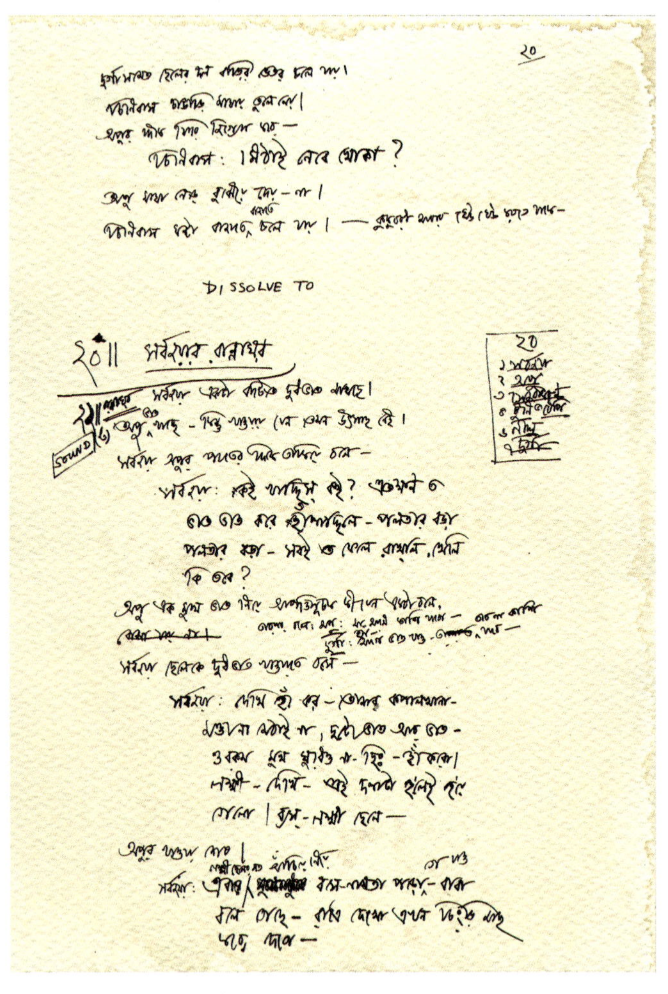
২০

DISSOLVE TO

২০॥

SOUND

Draft scenario 1

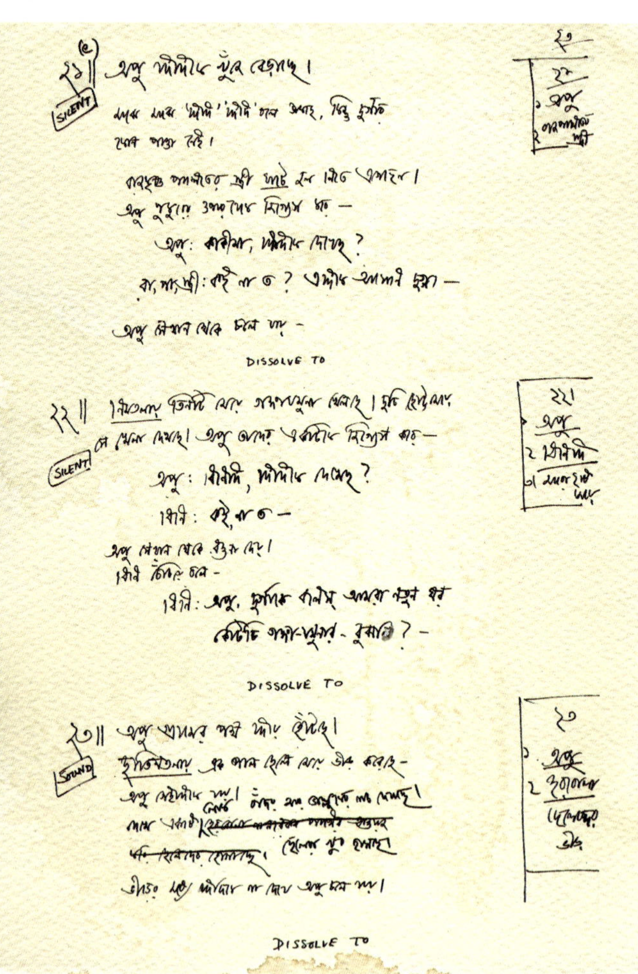
২১॥

SILENT

DISSOLVE TO

২২॥

SILENT

DISSOLVE TO

২৩॥

SOUND

DISSOLVE TO

Draft scenario 2

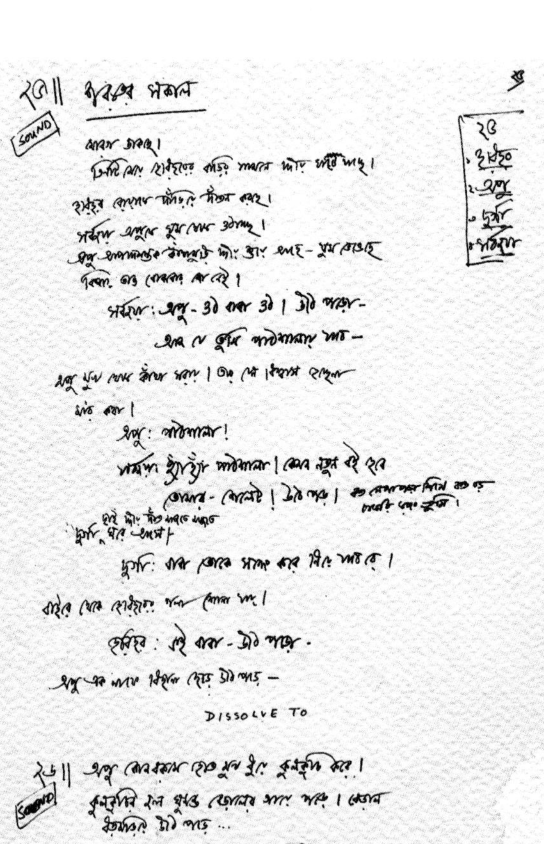

Draft scenario 3

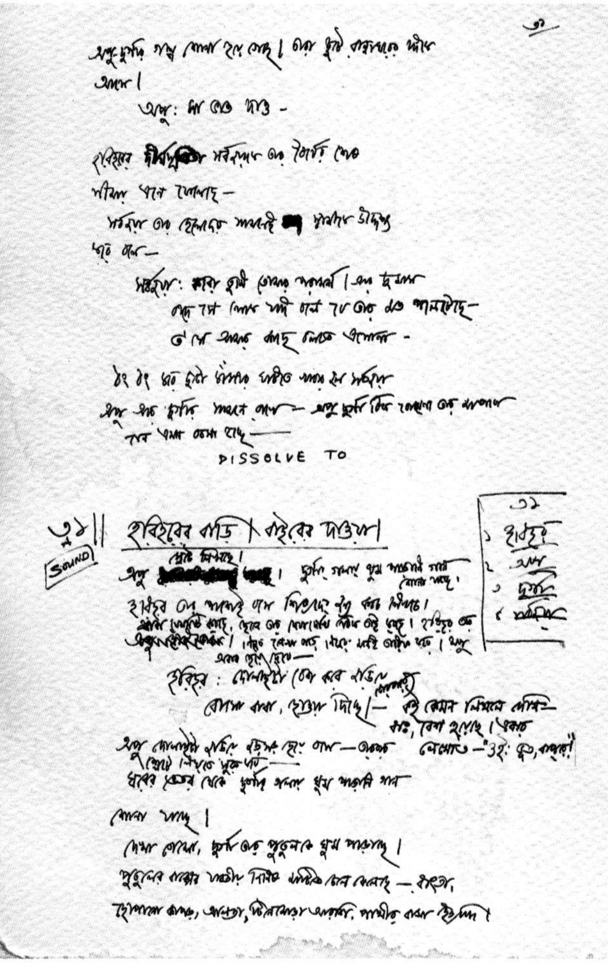

Draft scenario 4

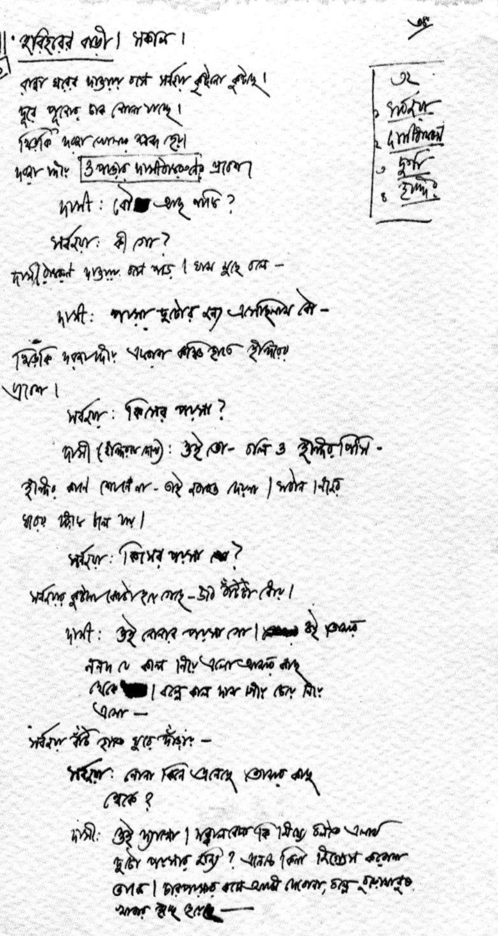

Draft scenario 5

DISSOLVE TO

Draft scenario 6

DISSOLVE TO

Draft scenario 7

Draft scenario 8

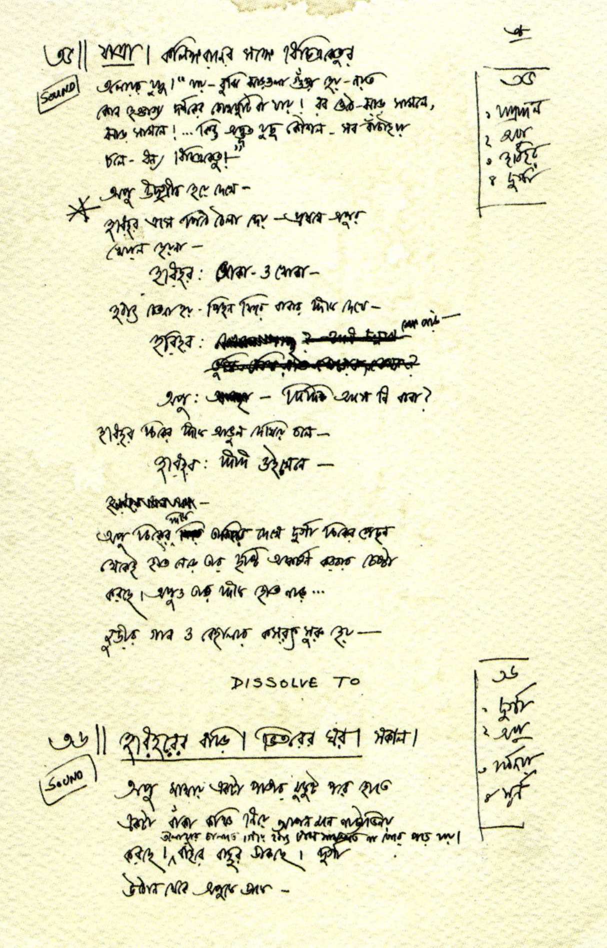

Draft scenario 9

THE LEGAL CONTRACT

AN AGREEMENT made this Twelfth day of April, Nineteen Hundred and Fifty-Four between Srimati ... Station Road, Barrackpore, 24 Parganas, who is the legal copyright owner of the work entitled PATHER PANCHALI by the late Bibhuti Bhusan Banerjee, hereinafter called the Licensor of the first part and Satyajit Ray, Proprietor of Darpan Kathachitra, Motion Picture Producers, of 31A Lake Avenue, Calcutta 26, hereinafter called the Producer of the other part, whereby it is mutually agreed as follows:

1) The Licensor grants to the Producer for the consideration hereinafter mentioned the rights of filming Pather Panchali in Bengali language.

2) The Producer agrees to pay to the Licensor a total sum of Rupees Ten Thousand only which is to be paid as follows : (a) A sum of Rupees ~~Three~~ Five Thousand is to be paid within three weeks of signing this contract, and (b) the remaining sum of Rupees ~~Seven~~ Five Thousand is to be paid within thirty days of release of the film for exhibition.

The producer agrees to complete the production for exhibition by December 31, 1957

4) The film is to be produced in Bengali language only. The Licensor withholds the rights for other Indian languages. Should a sub-titled version of the film be made in any non-Indian language for exhibition outside India and should any financial transaction take place for such purpose, the Licensor shall have the right to receive a ~~share of ten per cent for each of such transaction~~ separate agreement for this purpose.

5) The film production is to be an honest and true version of the work Pather Panchali as written by the late Bibhuti Bhusan Banerjee, and the producer shall not introduce any such topic or situation which shall distort the true spirit of the literary work.

6) The Licensor shall be responsible for any action of Libel or Infringement of copyright and shall indemnify and reimburse the Producer for any damages, costs or charges which they may reasonably incur or be called upon to pay in respect thereof

7) This agreement is to remain in force for a period of ~~ten~~ Eight years, after which the Licensor will have the right to grant permission for another production in Bengali language, if the Licensor so desires.

8) Failure to comply with any of the above conditions will render the contract null and void.

Rama Banerjee Satyajit Ray

WITNESS Dilip K. Gupta 10/2 Elgin Road

The contract signed between Bibhutibhushan Bandyopadhyay's wife and Satyajit Ray, acquiring the rights to make a film based on the novel

STATEMENT ON THE APU TRILOGY

Statement on the Apu Trilogy

The three films of the Apu Trilogy – Pather Panchali, Aparajito & The World of Apu – were based on two novels by one of the finest novelists of Bengal – Bibhutibhusan Banerji. The first novel – Pather Panchali, won immediate acclaim on publication for its lyricism, humanism & its remarkably authentic depiction of life in rural Bengal in the 3rd decade of the present century.

As one born and bred in the city, I had no contact with the village; but the novel was something like an encyclopaedia of rural life. This was proved beyond doubt when we actually started shooting the first film on rural locations.

While I learnt a lot about the craft of filmmaking

2

from watching Hollywood films of the 40's & 50's, my primary influences when I started my first film were Jean Renoir & the De Sica of Bicycle Thief & Umberto D. And yet, soon after I started shooting, I realised that the form, rhythm & texture of my film would derive from elements which were deeply rooted in my own culture, which had little to do with the culture of France or Italy.

When I was at work on Pather Panchali, I had no thought of making a Trilogy. After the world-wide success of the film, I decided to continue with the Apu story – still not thinking in terms of a Trilogy. It was in Venice in 1957, at the Press Conference after the screening of Aparajito, that I was asked if I had a Trilogy in mind. I found myself saying 'yes' –

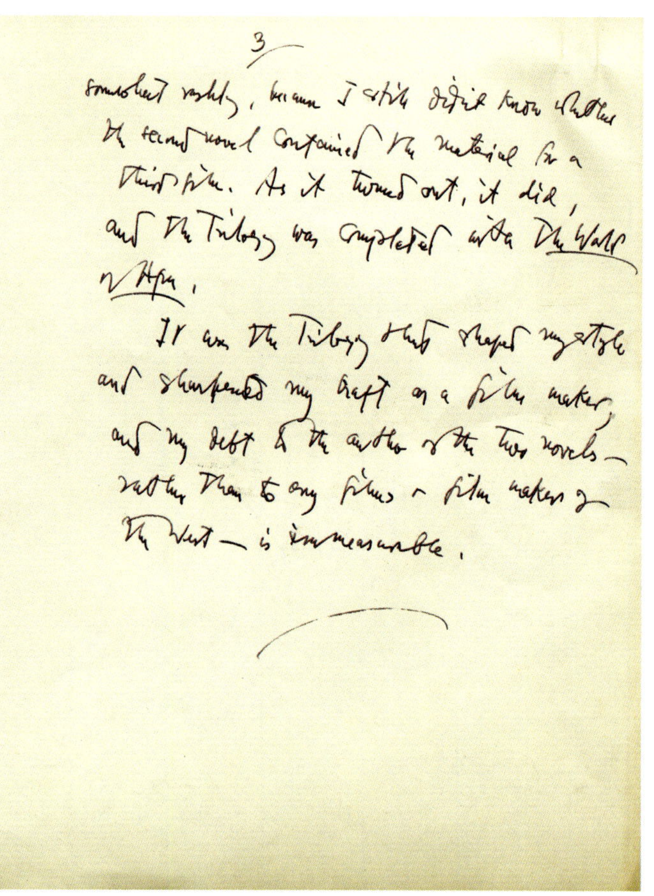

3

somewhat rashly, because I still didn't know whether the second novel contained the material for a third film. As it turned out, it did, and the Trilogy was completed with The World of Apu.

It was the Trilogy that shaped my style and sharpened my craft as a film maker, and my debt to the author of the two novels – rather than to any films or film makers of the West – is immeasurable.

Satyajit Ray's handwritten statement on the trilogy

AAM AANTIR BHENPU

Aam Aantir Bhenpu is the title of a children's edition of Bibhutibhushan Bandyopadhyay's epic novel *Pather Panchali*. Satyajit Ray made not only the jacket design but did the illustrations for the book as well. It was first published on 22 September 1944 by Signet Press.

ADVERTISEMENTS

THE STATESMAN FRIDAY AUGUST 26 1955

"The Shop At Sly Corner"

Western Film Review

CHASING MEN & TIGERS IN BURMA JUNGLES

INDIAN FILMS

Beware Toffee-Eaters

"KUNDAN" MAINTAINS HIGH STANDARD

NOTES ON INDIAN FILMS

OPENS TODAY!

KALO BOU

UTTARA . PURABI . UJJALA

LAUGHTER ON THE WINGS OF MUSIC!

NAQAD NARAYAN

FROM FRIDAY 2nd SEPT. at YOUR FAVOURITE THEATRES.

BETTER BEYOND EXPECTATIONS!

KUNDAN

SOHRAB MODI

ROXY . PRABHAT . RUPALI . PURNASREE . PARK SHOW . MENOKA

ELITE

VAN HEFLIN THE RAID

TODAY

JALWA

J—A—N—A—T—A

GRACE . ANJAN . KHANNA

NAAZ . PARAMOUNT . DIPTI

BASUSREE . BINA . CHAYA . SREE

Newspaper advertisement along with an interesting write-up, 'Notes on Indian Films', published in *The Statesman*, Calcutta, on 26 August 1955

THE STATESMAN FRIDAY SEPTEMBER 23 1955

NEW EMPIRE

REGAL

GLOBE

MINERVA

THE PRODIGAL

M-E-T-R-O

PRINCES

Scherazade

AZAAD

MUNNA

KUNDAN

MAXIM'S

Radio Programmes

Ask for... KEVENTERS the BETTER BUTTER

The Weather

PROTECT YOUR CHILD FROM ILLNESS

with this two-fold nourishment

SCOTT'S Emulsion

fully as good as you expect them to be

Private Reserve

RED CROSS BABY SHOW

RAJ BHAVAN, CALCUTTA

The Best Ever

DUI BON

CHITRA . INDIRA

BASUSREE . BINA . CHAYA

SEE how pure it is!

FEEL how good it is!

Pears SOAP

THE ORIGINAL GLYCERINE BEAUTY SOAP

An innovative newspaper advertisement published in *The Statesman*, Calcutta, on 23 September 1955

FRIDAY, **Hindusthan Standard** SEPTEMBER 2, 1955

Stage and Screen

PICK YOUR PICTURES

Reviewed by EMBEE

PATHER PANCHALI
(Govt. of West Bengal)

Let it be said quite clearly, and right at the outset, that this is no ordinary film we are reviewing. The caution is necessary, because so extravagant is the use of superlatives in film writing in general that words, adjectives in particular, have had their full meaning corroded away, as if by inflation. Every word in this review is to be taken at its full value.

This is the first Indian film which is Indian in every inch. We emphasise this aspect not because it has no universal appeal; it has, and that because it is truly Indian, but because this film is a truer picture of life in an Indian village than any we have seen. The story is well known, it relates to a Bengal village which is dying out—the sort of village we have all seen and turned away from. It is to such a spot that the young director, Satyajit Roy, has taken his camera, his seeing eye, his feeling heart, and his very capable hands. The result is a film of exquisite beauty, and it is, in the fullest sense of the term, a work of art—a thing we would not say about many films made anywhere.

Arundhati Mukherjee in her latest stellar triumph in "Godhuli," releasing today.

As has been said once before in this column, it is not in drama that the Bengali film will ever come near its foreign competitors. Life in this part of the world is harsh, painful—but rarely violent. It is the emotions which are occasionally, and only occasionally, violent. What is more in tune with the plastic soil of Bengal is the poetic quality of our nature, human and physical. It is this poetic quality of our landscape, mental and physical which has been caught triumphantly by Director Roy. The characters in the film—Indir Thakrun, Apu, Durga, Sarvajaya and others—are all portrayed beautifully, and Durga is just superb—and having said that, we will go on to add that never is the human element allowed to dominate the film. That would indeed have been false, for in life too the characters are dominated by nature. They are, oftener than not, objects rather than subjects. But all that is sociology.

Director Roy's approach is poetic and artistic. Some of the compositions, that quivering lotus in the pond on the eve of the rains, for instance, are like painting. The conception of the entire reel covering the onset of the rains in a Bengal village is poetic and anyone who has known how the rains change the face of the whole countryside will re-live that unforgettable experience in this film. A dying Bengal village has never before come to life as it has done in this unique, yes unique, creation. *Pather Panchali* is a thing of beauty from beginning to end, and let us put it quite bluntly that if for any reason this film should not receive the universal acclamation it deserves (in terms of critical praise and in those of box office returns), we will have forfeited our right to ask for a good film again.

Some misconceptions remain to be removed. The film is sponsored by the Government of West Bengal. But the latter, very wisely, refrains from interfering with the film. There is no propaganda, except what there is in the theme. The propaganda is that it is only a dead heart which will not, after seeing this film, want to do something for India's villages. But let it be clearly understood that the Government has not imposed any of its propaganda stuff on the film which is as its director conceived it.

Secondly, let no one fall into the error of thinking that *Pather Panchali* is intended for long-haired, unwashed, coffee-drinking intellectuals who form cinema societies and do not pay the monthly subscription in time. This is a people's film, if ever there has been one. There are certainly scenes and suggestions which can be appreciated the more by those who have some knowledge of film technique—those who have read Eisenstein and seen Flaherty—but there is nothing at all which cannot be enjoyed by exactly those people whose life the film deals with. "Deal with" did we say? That is a sordid phrase. The film is a piece of poetry, dedicated to the deathless spirit of Bengal and it is a poem which can be heard and recited by every Bengali. And, being Bengali, it is bound to conquer the rest of India and the whole world. This film, let us aver, marks the Indian film's coming of age. We salute Satyajit Roy and all his comrades who have produced this superb film. Yes, superb.

D.R.M.

FOREIGN PICTURES

AT METRO

THE PRODIGAL

M-G-M has expanded the well-known parable of the Prodigal Son into a spectacle of pagan splendour, which ranks with the very best that the company has turned out in this line. Cinemascope and colour add their own charm to the production.

It's all about Micah, son of a prosperous Jewish farmer, who falls into disgrace through his uncontrollable infatuation for Samarra, alluring pagan priestess. The period is 70 years before Christ and the action takes place in Damascus where pagan worship flourishes. Micah's downfall and the struggle between Samarra's love for him and her fidelity to her gods are excellently offset against the revolt of the starving populace against the tyrannical regime of Nahreeb. These make for a motion picture which combines a passionate love story, surging dramatic action and breathtaking spectacle.

Lana Turner brings a flaming intensity to the role of Samarra, while Edmund Purdom is dominant and persuasive as the Prodigal, forced to taste the dregs of life before he can prove his worth. Louis Calhern, in one of his rare villainous roles, makes a despicable figure of Nahreeb, the greedy and unscrupulous high priest of Baal. Among the supporting players, James Mitchell, Taina Elg, Audrey Dalton, Walter Hampden and Francis L. Sullivan are most prominent.

AT GLOBE

JUDGMENT OF PARIS

This Continental production in Technicolor recreates the story of Helen of Troy and weaves drama with her tragic and fatal love for Paris.

Hedy Lamarr shares stellar honours with Europe's male heart-throb, Massimo Serato, and the two excellently imbue themselves with the spirit of their respective parts—as Helen and Paris. Robert Beatty plays Helen's revengeful husband Menelaus with appropriate villainy while Cathy O'Donnell and Alba Arnova, well-known Continental stars, contribute outstanding performances in support.

Produced on a lavish scale the film makes cinemagoers feel that they are participating in the violence and passion that arise from the ill-fated romance of Helen and Paris. Marc Allegret's imaginative direction leaves its distinctive stamp on this spectacular production.

AT ELITE

THERE'S NO BUSINESS LIKE SHOW BUSINESS

If you have any doubt about the truthful import of the title, just go and see this magnificent musical in Cinemascope. It is

Chitra is the glamorous heroine of Shah Pictures' "Roop Basant", releasing today.

Far Left: Newspaper review published in the 'Pick Your Pictures' section of the *Hindusthan Standard*, 2 September 1955
Left: A closer look at the review

LETTERS TO RAY

THE MUSEUM OF MODERN ART
11 WEST 53 STREET, NEW YORK 19, N. Y.

VIA AIR MAIL

Mr. Satyajit Ray
31 A Lake Avenue
Calcutta 26, India

THE MUSEUM OF MODERN ART

NEW YORK 19

11 WEST 53rd STREET
TELEPHONE: CIRCLE 5-8900
CABLES: MODERNART, NEW-YORK

MONROE WHEELER
DIRECTOR OF EXHIBITIONS AND PUBLICATIONS

September 30, 1955

Dear Satyajit:

I am overjoyed to hear of the success of your film in Calcutta! This is a success you richly deserve for your long patience and perserverance. I hope you succeed in obtaining the future commercial rights. In any case, this triumph should make it easier for you to obtain backing for your next film.

Can you let us know when you will be able to send us the revised version for our Film Library? Please remember that we are prepared to do everything in our power to launch it here.

With renewed felicitations and warm remembrances, I am,

Faithfully yours,

Monroe.

Monroe Wheeler

Mr. Satyajit Ray
31 A, Lake Avenue
Calcutta 26, India

MW:ak

THE MUSEUM OF MODERN ART

NEW YORK 19

11 WEST 53rd STREET
TELEPHONE: CIRCLE 5-8900
CABLES: MODERNART, NEW-YORK

MONROE WHEELER
DIRECTOR OF EXHIBITIONS AND PUBLICATIONS

January 19, 1956

Dear Satyajit:

We showed your APU AND DURGA the other day to Mr. Edward Harrison, who is one of the top distributors of foreign films in America. He was extremely enthusiastic about it and would like to distribute it in America on the usual basis of sharing all profits equally with the owner. This brings up the question -- who is the owner -- and with whom should Mr. Harrison negotiate? He tells me it is customary to get a negative from which copies can be made, and insert the English subtitles here, according to your instructions, when the duplicates are made.

I hope the film has had further success in India and that you have now embarked upon another.

With all best wishes, I am,

Sincerely yours,

Monroe.

Monroe Wheeler

Mr. Satyajit Ray
31 A Lake Avenue
Calcutta 26, India

MW:ak

Above: Letter from Monroe Wheeler introducing Edward Harrison who eventually became the distributor of *Pather Panchali* in the USA

Left: Letter from Monroe Wheeler, Director of Exhibitions and Publications, The Museum of Modern Art, New York

BRADBURY
10265 CHEVIOT DRIVE
LOS ANGELES 64, CALIF.

T.5¢

MR. SATYAJIT RAY
3 Lake Temple Road
Calcutta 29, INDIA.

Via Ai

April 5th, 1963

Dear Mr. Ray:
At last, I have seen the APU Trilogy and come away with a sense of your life and the life of those around you so very far away. Above all, you have made me proud once more of the uses of cinema, for we are involved, those of us who love motion-picture making, in working with what I call The Empathy Machine. To let a man know what it is to be a woman, to allow a woman to know what it is to be a man, to be a child again while grown old, to be old when young, to sense a Jew's position while born a Moslem, to be sick when well, and to be made well in the midst of sickness, these are all proud and exciting challenges that cinema offers us. This is the long way around to telling you I know some small bit of India now because of you, and I hope one day to offer you a piece of my America to examine and know. Thank you for this fine experience and helping me to look out through the eyes of APU for a little while. Yours with wishes for a creative future.

Ray Bradbury

ROBERT FLAHERTY FOUNDATION, INC.

R.F.D. 1, BOX 94, BRATTLEBORO, VERMONT TELEPHONE: ALpine 4-2615

January 12, 1959

Dear Satyajit Ray,

This joint letter is to tell you how very happy we both were to receive your kind New Year wishes and to know that the third film of your Trilogy is coming along so well. It is good that you have been able to work on it uninterruptedly since your return from Brussels. You probably hear from Ed Harrison every now and then, so that there may be no need to tell you of the very successful run "Pather Panchali" has been enjoying at the Fifth Avenue Playhouse; indeed it is still playing there. All of your friends here are delighted that Bosley Crowther has been made to eat the words of his condescending, insensitive and shallow review. We have heard that Ed Harrison intends to open "The Unvanquished" soon.

As you know, we would dearly love to acquire for the Foundation a 16 mm print of "Pather Panchali" without the subtitles. We telephoned Ed Harrison to find out whether there might be a negative or fine-grain in New York without the subtitles, but apparently there never was one in this country. Ed, who most generously presented to the Foundation the original 35 mm print of "Pather Panchali", which is without titles, has no objection to our acquiring a 16 mm print if we are able to do so, since he knows that our use of it would not in any way conflict with the theatrical or non-theatrical distribution of the film. Incidentally, the 35 mm print he gave us is a beautiful one. We got a laugh on reading the label the storage company had put on the shipping cases. They had translated "Pather Panchali" into "Panther's Paradise"!

Could you tell us to whom we might write in connection with this 16 mm untitled print? We would of course gladly pay the laboratory and shipping costs.

Again we want to tell you how wonderful it was to have you with us here last summer. Your presence, with the two films, made the seminar the best and most memorable of all we have so far had. We all hope that, seminar or no seminar, you will visit us in Vermont again before long.

All our best wishes to you for the New Year, and for the success of "The Unvanquished" and the third film of your Trilogy.

As ever, sincerely,

Frances Flaherty
David

Satyajit Ray, Esq.
31-A Lake Avenue
Calcutta 26, India.

Above: Letter from Robert Flaherty Foundation enquiring about acquiring a 16 mm print of *Pather Panchali*

Left: Letter from Ray Bradbury, author of the cult novel *Fahrenheit 451*

Jean Renoir
1273 Leona Drive
Beverly Hills, Calif.

PRAY FOR PEACE

Redirect.

Mr. Manick Roy
INDIA.

C/O RAI J. N. ROY CHOWDHURY BA.
P.O NIMTITA.
MUSHIDABAD.

1273 Leona Drive
Beverly Hills, California.

February 7, 1957

Dear Manick Roy:

I knew that you had made "Pather Panchali" and that Banzi had collaborated with you. I didn't know however that Mitra was also in the film. Before writing to you I wanted to see the picture. But time is passing, and up to now I had no occasion to attend a projection. If there is a print in Hollywood, please tell me the name and the address of the person in charge of it. I heard so many good things about your work and the artistic achievements of your partners that it makes me anxious to know it.

All my warmest congratulations for your sucess. Please convey my compliments to Banzi and Mitra.

My wife and I send our best regards to your wife and to yourself, and also all our good wishes to your baby.

Sincerely,

Jean Renoir

Jean Renoir

Letter from Jean Renoir wishing Satyajit Ray, Bansi Chandragupta ('Banzi') and Subrata Mitra ('Mitra'). Bansi Chandragupta was part of Renoir's crew for *The River*. Mitra was an observer on the sets. Ray dropped in occasionally to watch Renoir shoot.

Air Mail

Sri. Manik Ray.
~~c/o Clarion Advertising~~.
~~5, Council House Street~~,
31 A Lake Avenue
Calcutta 26
~~Calcutta~~
~~West Bengal~~.
INDIA.

MOAT HOUSE, IVYCHURCH, ROMNEY MARSH, KENT.
Telephone: BROOKLAND 259.

16·xii·57.

Dear Manik,

We have just been delighted with an extract from your film on the B.B.C. Television, and have heard of the Award at the Venice Festival. It is to be shewn shortly in London. The award was for the "most human story of the year" - but what about the human story behind the film? I cannot tell you how delighted I am that your artistic integrity and determination in the face of such heartbreaking setbacks has received the reward - if not financial, at least - or rather better - that of international recognition. Perhaps I am rather pleased with myself as the opinion I formed when I saw the rushes has been confirmed!!

We often talk about you, and wonder how you are progressing - I hope you are on the way to making your fortune, or whatever your ambition may be.

If you should be in touch with Shama Ghosh and O.C. Ganguli, please give them my kindest regards.

My wife joins me in sending you our very best wishes, and we hope one day we may see you again. Should you come to England at any time, do please get in touch with me.

Yours sincerely.

J.B.R. Nicholson.

Above: Ray working at D.J. Keymer & Associates
Far Left: Letter to Ray from J.B.R. Nicholson who was his immediate boss when Ray worked at D.J. Keymer & Associates as art director
Left: Sketch of J.B.R. Nicholson by Ray

ACCOLADES

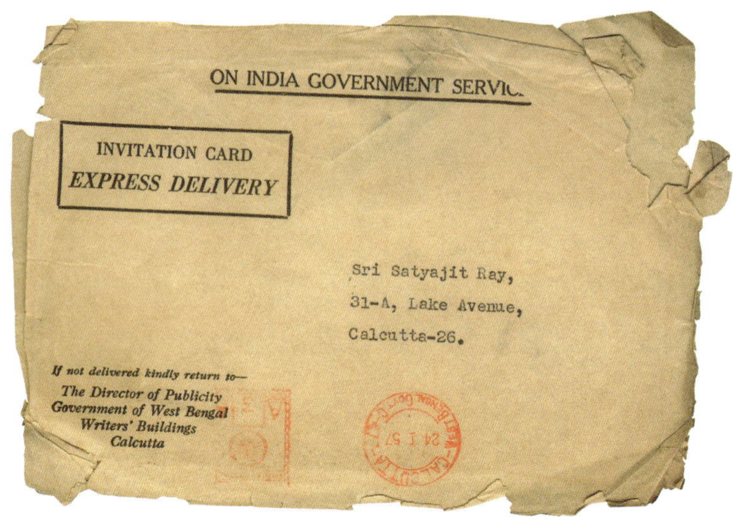

ON INDIA GOVERNMENT SERVIC

INVITATION CARD
EXPRESS DELIVERY

Sri Satyajit Ray,
31-A, Lake Avenue,
Calcutta-26.

If not delivered kindly return to—
The Director of Publicity
Government of West Bengal
Writers' Buildings
Calcutta

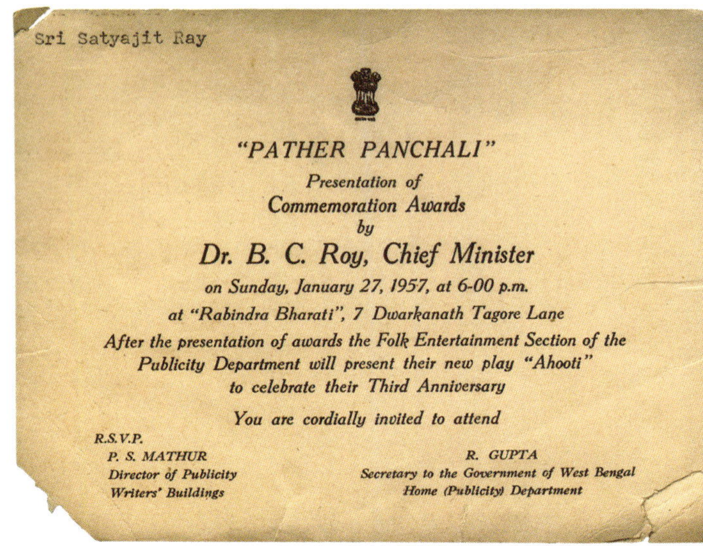

Sri Satyajit Ray

"PATHER PANCHALI"

Presentation of
Commemoration Awards
by
Dr. B. C. Roy, Chief Minister
on Sunday, January 27, 1957, at 6-00 p.m.
at "Rabindra Bharati", 7 Dwarkanath Tagore Lane
After the presentation of awards the Folk Entertainment Section of the Publicity Department will present their new play "Ahooti" to celebrate their Third Anniversary

You are cordially invited to attend

R.S.V.P.
P. S. MATHUR
Director of Publicity
Writers' Buildings

R. GUPTA
Secretary to the Government of West Bengal
Home (Publicity) Department

Above: Letter from the Government of West Bengal, inviting Satyajit Ray for an awards ceremony

Right: Chief Minister Dr Bidhan Chandra Roy felicitating Ray

Chunibala Devi being felicitated by Dr Roy

The cast and crew of *Pather Panchali* with Dr Roy. **From left to right:** Chunibala Devi, Bansi Chandragupta, Karuna Banerjee, Subir Banerjee, Satyajit Ray, Kanu Banerjee, Uma Dasgupta, Dr Bidhan Chandra Roy, Runki Banerjee and Subrata Mitra.

COMMEMORATIVE STAMPS

तकनीकी आंकड़े
TECHNICAL DATA

जारी करने की तारीख Date of Issue	11/1/1994
मूल्यवर्ग Denomination	1100 पैसे तथा 600 पैसे 1100 (P) and 600 (P)
कुल आकार Overall size	10.50 × 3.50 से.मी.
मुद्रण आकार Printing size	10.15 × 3.15 से.मी.
प्रति शीट संख्या Number per issue sheet	12 set सेट
रंग Colour	बहुरंगी Multicolour
छिद्रण Perforation	13 × 13
कागज़ Paper	विदेशी बिना जल चिह्न वाला फोटोग्रेव्योर अँडेसिव कोटेड कागज, 50.8 से.मी. × 53.5 से.मी. आकार में। Imported un-water marked adhesive photogravure coated paper in size 50.8 cms × 53.5 cms.
मुद्रण प्रक्रिया Printing process	फोटोग्रेव्योर Photogravure process
टाइप-फेस Type face	रे-रोमन Ray Roman
मुद्रित डाक-टिकटों की संख्या दस लाख Number Printed	one million
मुद्रण Printed	भारत प्रतिभूति मुद्रणालय India Security Press

Above: The commemorative stamp issued by Cine Central, Calcutta, to celebrate the twenty-fifth year of *Pather Panchali*

Left: The commemorative stamp issued by the Department of Posts on 11 January 1994

Celebrating *Pather Panchali*: A Night to Remember

The Criterion Collection

The MoMA lobby displaying the poster of the restored Apu Trilogy

Pather Panchali had its first screening at the Museum of Modern Art (MoMA) in New York City on 3 May 1955, and on 4 May 2015, almost exactly sixty years later, MoMA screened this landmark debut film by Satyajit Ray in a new restoration undertaken by the Criterion Collection, in collaboration with L'Immagine Ritrovata in Bologna, Italy, and the Academy Film Archive at the Academy of Motion Picture Arts and Sciences in Los Angeles, California. The occasion attracted both long-time fans of the film and newcomers to Apu, including film-makers, musicians and artists such as Joel Coen, Wes Anderson, Jim Jarmusch, Laurie Anderson, Ken Burns, Alice Waters and Noah Baumbach. What made the evening all the more special for everyone in attendance was the presence of Satyajit Ray's son Sandip, Sandip's wife Lolita, and Shampa (Runki) Srivastava (formerly Banerjee), who plays the young Durga at the start of the film and whose mother performs as Apu and Durga's mother. As Sandip shared with the audience prior to the screening, 'I am envious of those who will be seeing the film for the first time.'

Sandip Ray addressing the audience

In the 1950s, for a first-time film-maker from India to premiere his film in New York was a rare event, and for Ray, it proved fortuitous. When Ray was in the midst of producing *Pather Panchali*, Monroe Wheeler, a curator from MoMA, was travelling in India and visited Ray at work. Wheeler was in search of images to include in Edward Steichen's international photography exhibition *The Family of Man*. Ray projected for Wheeler some recently shot scenes from his film, and for the exhibition, the curator chose a frame that depicted Apu's mother and sister getting Apu ready for school. Months later, film-maker John Huston, who was in India scouting for one of his films, paid Ray a visit on Wheeler's behalf, to see how his film was coming along. Huston reported back in a letter to Wheeler that he 'recognized the footage as the work of a great film-maker'. Upon reading Huston's praise, Wheeler invited Ray to screen *Pather Panchali*

Film-makers Ken Burns and Jim Jarmusch

From left to right: The Criterion Collection president Peter Becker, and film-makers Noah Baumbach, Joel Coen, Wes Anderson and Jim Jarmusch

Musician/film-maker Laurie Anderson and chef/author Alice Waters

as part of his large-scale exhibition *Textiles and Ornaments of India*. It is the anniversary of this screening that the Criterion Collection, a rapt audience, and all who helped to restore the film celebrated last spring.

The journey to restore *Pather Panchali* and Ray's subsequent features *Aparajito* and *Apur Sansar* – which together form the Apu Trilogy – began back in 1992, when the Academy presented Ray with an honorary Oscar for lifetime achievement. When sourcing material from Ray's films for the Academy Awards ceremony, telecast producers were dismayed by the poor condition of the existing prints. The following year, after Ray's death, a project was initiated to restore many of his films, including those in the Apu Trilogy.

In 1993, several of the film-maker's original negatives were shipped to Henderson's Film Laboratories in London. In July, a massive nitrate fire at the lab spread to the film vaults, destroying more than twenty-five original negatives of important British classics and burning several Ray films, including the original negatives of the Apu Trilogy. Any ashes, fragments or film cans that could be identified as belonging to Ray's films were sent to the Academy Film Archive, but the trilogy's negatives were deemed unprintable. There were no technologies available at the time capable of fully restoring such badly damaged film elements.

Wes Anderson and Sandip Ray

Joel Coen, Sandip Ray and the Criterion Collection president Peter Becker

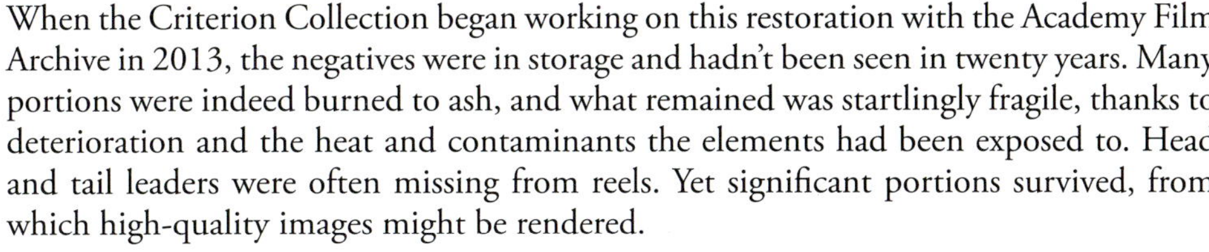

When the Criterion Collection began working on this restoration with the Academy Film Archive in 2013, the negatives were in storage and hadn't been seen in twenty years. Many portions were indeed burned to ash, and what remained was startlingly fragile, thanks to deterioration and the heat and contaminants the elements had been exposed to. Head and tail leaders were often missing from reels. Yet significant portions survived, from which high-quality images might be rendered.

No commercial laboratory would handle this material, so it was entrusted to L'Immagine Ritrovata in Bologna, one of the world's premier restoration facilities. There, technicians successfully rehydrated the brittle film using a special solution (one part glycerol, one part acetone, three parts water). Scanning tests determined that pin-registered wet-gate scans yielded the best results. Technicians then set about physically repairing the elements. This meant almost a thousand hours of meticulous hand labour, which even included rebuilding the perforation holes on the sides of the film and removing melted tape and glue. Using fine-grain masters and duplicate negatives preserved by Janus Films, the Academy, the Harvard Film Archive and the British Film Institute, the technicians found excellent replacements for the unusable or missing sections of the original negatives. In the end, 40 per cent of *Pather Panchali* and over 60 per cent of *Aparajito* were restored directly from the original negatives. The two surviving reels of *Apur Sansar* were too damaged to be used in the restoration, so all of that film was restored from a fine-grain master and a duplicate negative.

Over the course of nearly six months of steady work, the Criterion Collection restoration lab handled the digital restoration, including eliminating dirt, debris, warps and cracks. Emphasis was placed on retaining the look and character of the original material, preferring when necessary to leave damage rather than over-process digital images that might lose the grain and feel of film.

All in all, the restoration of the Apu Trilogy was years in the making. The return of these films to MoMA and a wider release in theatres across the US and Canada marked a triumph for the archivists and members of the preservation community who had had the foresight and faith to protect these vital treasures of world cinema even when all seemed lost.

Cast and Crew

Produced by the Government of West Bengal. **Script and Direction:** Satyajit Ray. **Based on a novel by** Bibhutibhushan Bandyopadhyay. **Cinematography:** Subrata Mitra. **Art Direction:** Bansi Chandragupta. **Music:** Ravi Shankar. **Editing:** Dulal Dutta. **Sound:** Bhupen Ghosh and Satyen Chatterjee. **Production Control:** Anil Choudhury.

Duration: 115 min.

Assistants

Direction: Shanti Kumar Chatterjee, Ashis Burman, Subir Hazra. **Cinematography:** Dinen Gupta, Nemai Ray, Biren Bhattacharya, Soumendu Roy. **Art Direction:** Suresh Chandra, Surat Bar, Dibakar Dutta. **Editing:** Sukumar Sengupta, Tapeshwar Prasad, Harinarayan Mukherjee. **Production Control:** Suren Sahu, Satya, Natabar, Badal, Dulal.

Actors

Kanu Banerjee (Harihar), Karuna Banerjee (Sarbajaya), Subir Banerjee (Apu), Uma Dasgupta (Durga), Chunibala Devi (Indir Thakrun), Runki Banerjee (little Durga), Reba Devi (Sejo Thakrun), Aparna Devi (Nilmani's wife), Tulsi Chakrabarti (Prasanna, schoolteacher), Binoy Mukherjee (Baidyanath Majumdar), Haren Banerjee (Srinibas, the sweetmeat peddler), Harimohan Nag (Doctor), Haridhan Nag (Chakrabarty), Nibhanani Devi (Dasi Thakrun), Kshirod Roy (Priest), Rama Ganguli (Ranu), Tenpi (Manju), Satu (Shyamal), Tuni (Putulrani), Punti (Papiya), Bini (Aparna).

Distribution: Aurora Films Corporation Private Ltd.

Date of release: 26 August 1955, at Calcutta's Basusree, Bina, Chhaya, Shree and other movie theatres.

Select Awards

President's Gold and Silver Medals, New Delhi, 1955

Best Human Document, Cannes, 1956

Diploma of Merit, Edinburgh, Scotland, 1956

Vatican Award, Rome, 1956

Golden Carbao, Rome, 1956

Best Film and Best Director, San Francisco, 1957

Selznick Golden Laurel, Berlin, 1957

Best Film, Vancouver, Canada, 1958

Critics' Award: Best Film, Stratford, Canada, 1958

Cultural Award: Best Foreign Film, New York, 1959

Kinema Jumpo Award: Best Foreign Film, Tokyo, 1966

Bodil Award: Best Non-European Film of the Year, Denmark, 1966

Society for the Preservation of Satyajit Ray Archives
Preserving a Priceless Legacy

Sometime after Satyajit Ray passed away, a number of actors and public personalities – Amitabh Bachchan and the late Ismail Merchant among them – teamed up to form what is today the Society for the Preservation of Satyajit Ray Archives (formerly Society for the Preservation of Satyajit Ray Films). Popularly known as Satyajit Ray Society or just Ray Society, it was founded in 1994 with the objective of restoring and preserving the priceless legacies left by the master director as also disseminating his work worldwide.

Ray Restoration

When Ray breathed his last in 1992, negatives and prints of many of his films, especially those of his early classics, were in a precarious state. David H. Shepard, a noted film preservationist in California, came to India to examine the original negatives of the Ray films. He found the negatives of eighteen of his films in 'tatters'. Restoration of Ray films was the Society's primary concern at the time. It went into a tie-up with the Los Angeles-based Academy of Motion Picture Arts and Sciences, the hallowed institution which had conferred the Oscar for Lifetime Achievement on Ray. So far, a majority of the maestro's thirty-six-film oeuvre has been restored at the Academy Archive. More are waiting to mount the restoration anvil.

Ray Archives

Apart from his films, Ray left behind an astonishingly wide artistic universe comprising scripts, storyboards, posters, set, costume and book jacket designs, literary manuscripts, illustrations, music notations, advertisement artworks and so on. The Society has arguably the largest and most authentic archive on Ray in its custody. A veritable treasure trove, the Ray paper archive contains almost the entire creative output of his multifaceted genius. A large part of Ray's paper legacy has been restored under the supervision of Mike Wheeler, Senior Conservator (Paper Preservation) at the Victoria-Albert Museum, London, and is housed in his family home in Kolkata. The large personal library that Ray left and also his personal effects are being carefully preserved.

Publishing Ray Books

As part of its dissemination campaign, the Society has begun to publish books by and on Ray. It brought out *Deep Focus: Reflections on Cinema*, a collection of long-lost essays by Ray, in December 2011, in collaboration with HarperCollins *Publishers* India. In 2014, the Society published, again jointly with HarperCollins, *Satyajit Ray's Ravi Shankar*, a facsimile edition of the visual script that the master director did for his intended film on the sitar maestro. The Society brought out *Probandho Samagro*, a collection of Bengali articles by Ray, jointly with Ananda Publishers on 1 May 2015. More are in the pipeline.

Exhibitions and Film Shows

The Society has arranged quite a number of exhibitions of Ray's artworks as also festivals of his films at home and abroad. Some of the places where such shows and film retrospectives have taken place are Kolkata, Mumbai, Delhi, Toronto, Valladolid (Spain) and London.

Ray Memorial Lecture

The Society has been organizing lectures dedicated to Ray's memory delivered by distinguished film personalities for quite a few years. Javed Akhtar gave the first lecture in 2009, followed by Shyam Benegal (in 2012) and Naseeruddin Shah (in 2014). Soumitra Chattopadhyay delivered the next lecture on the eve of Ray's ninety-fourth birth anniversary on 1 May 2015. The Society also held a dialogue on the sixtieth anniversary of *Pather Panchali* in August 2015 with a glittering panel of speakers that included Aparna Sen, Dibakar Banerjee, Dileep Padgaonkar, Nandita Das, Sharmila Tagore, Shoojit Sircar, Sujoy Ghosh and Suman Mukhopadhyay. The seminar was moderated by Dhritiman Chaterji.

SOCIETY FOR THE PRESERVATION OF SATYAJIT RAY ARCHIVES
www.satyajitrayworld.com
satyajitraysociety@gmail.com

ACKNOWLEDGEMENTS

Sight & Sound, London, and Rob Winter and Isabel Stevens, its publisher and production editor, respectively

The Criterion Collection, New York, and Peter Becker and Abbey Lustgarten, its president and producer, respectively

The Anandabazar Patrika group (of dailies and magazines), Kolkata, and Shaktidas Roy, its librarian

The Statesman, Kolkata

Filmfare, Mumbai

Chitrabhas magazine, Kolkata, and Jyotiprakash Mitra, its editor

Uma Sen, Subir Banerjee, Soumendu Roy, the estates of Subrata Mitra, Dulal Dutta and Bansi Chandragupta

Riddhi Goswami

Pinaki De, for the extraordinary design in very little time

Adoor Gopalakrishnan

Lolita Ray

Aditi Nath Sarkar